British Terriers
Division I – English and Welsh
Division II – Scotch and Irish

by
J.Maxtee

Read Country Books
Home Farm
44 Evesham Road
Cookhill, Alcester
Warwickshire
B49 5lJ

www.readcountrybooks.com

ISBN No. 978-1-4067-9561-5

British Library Cataloguing-in-publication Data
A catalogue record for this book is available
from the British Library.

Read Country Books
Home Farm
44 Evesham Road
Cookhill, Alcester
Warwickshire
B49 5lJ

www.readcountrybooks.com

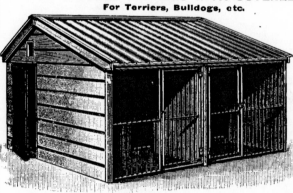

The Kennel Library.

BRITISH DOGS.

Their Points, Selection, and Show Preparation. Third Edition. By eminent specialists. Beautifully Illustrated. This is the fullest work on the various breeds of dogs kept in England. In one volume, *demy 8vo, cloth, price 12/6 nett, by post 13/-*.

PRACTICAL KENNEL MANAGE-MENT.

A Complete Treatise on the Proper Management of Dogs, for the Show Bench, the Field, or as Companions, with a chapter on Diseases—their Causes and Treatment. By well-known Specialists. Illustrated. *In cloth, price 10/6 nett, by post 11/-*.

DISEASES OF DOGS.

Their Causes, Symptoms, and Treatment; Modes of Administering Medicines; Treatment in cases of Poisoning, &c. For the use of Amateurs. By HUGH DALZIEL. Fourth Edition. Entirely Re-written and brought up to date. By ALEX. C. PIESSE, M.R.C.V.S. *Price 1/- nett, by post 1/2; in cloth, price 2/- nett, by post 2/3.*

BREAKING AND TRAINING DOGS.

Being Concise Directions for the proper education of Dogs, both for the Field and for Companions. Second Edition. By "PATHFINDER." Many new Illustrations. *In cloth, price 6/6 nett, by post 6/10.*

POPULAR DOG KEEPING:

Being a Handy Guide to the General Management and Training of all Kinds of Dogs for Companions and Pets. Third Edition. By J. MAXTEE. Illustrated. *Price 1/- nett, by post 1/2.*

THE FOX TERRIER.

Its Points, Breeding, Rearing, Preparing for Exhibition. Second Edition, Revised and brought up to date. Fully Illustrated. *Price 1/- nett, by post 1/2.*

THE COLLIE,

As a Show Dog, Companion, and Worker. Revised by J. MAXTEE. Third Edition. Illustrated. *Price 1/- nett, by post 1/2.*

THE GREYHOUND:

Its Points, Breeding, Rearing, Training, and Running. Second Edition, Revised and brought up to date by J. MAXTEE, assisted by T. B. RIXON. Illustrated. *Price 1/- nett, by post 1/2.*

THE WHIPPET OR RACE-DOG.

How to Breed, Rear, Train, Race, and Exhibit the Whippet, the Management of Race Meetings, and Original Plans of Courses. By FREEMAN LLOYD. Illustrated. *Price 1/- nett, by post 1/2.*

BREEDERS' AND EXHIBITORS' RECORD,

For the Registration of Particulars concerning Pedigree Stock of every Description. By W. K. TAUNTON. In three parts. *In cloth, price each 2/6 nett, or the set 6/- nett, by post 6/6.*
Part I., The Pedigree Record.   Part II., The Stud Record.
Part III., The Show Record.

London: L. UPCOTT GILL, Bazaar Buildings, Drury Lane, W.C.

Kennel Indispensables.

The Ideal Disinfectant

Famous as a cure for Mange, Eczema, Ringworm, and all other parasitic skin diseases.

A GRAND HAIR PRODUCER.

Destroys all insects such as fleas, lice, ticks, etc.

Sold in tins at 9d., 1/3, 2/- each; 6/- per gallon.
Free for P.O.

The Kennel, the Stable, the Poultry Yard kept sweet and healthy.
Ask for IZAL Veterinary Pamphlet.

IZAL Disinfectant Powder.

THE STRONGEST POWDER KNOWN.

In tins, 6d. and 1/- each; 50 lb. casks, 5/-. Free for P.O.

IZAL Soft Soap, *8d. per lb. Post free.*
IZAL Bar Soap. *8d. per lb. Post free.*

Special quotations for large lots.

NEWTON, CHAMBERS & Co., Ltd.,
THORNCLIFFE, NEAR SHEFFIELD.

BARNARDS LIMITED, NORWICH

IMPROVED RANGE OF KENNELS AND RUNS.
No. 347.

Each kennel, 6ft. wide, 5ft. deep. Runs, each 6ft. long, 6ft. wide, finished in the very best style.

One House and Run	£7	10	0
Two Houses and Runs	12	15	0
Three ditto	18	18	0
Six ditto	35	0	0

Carriage Paid.

NEW PORTABLE KENNEL AND RUN.
Registered Design.
No. 345.

3ft. 6in. wide, 8ft. long, 4ft. high	£4	5	0
4ft. wide, 9ft. 6in. long, 5ft. high	5	10	0
5ft. wide, 12ft. long, 5ft. high	7	10	0

Carriage Paid.

IMPROVED KENNEL.
No. 348.

AWARDED GOLD MEDAL SCHEVENINGEN, 1901 and 1906.

For Terriers ...	£1	7	6
For Collies, &c.	2	5	6
For Mastiffs ...	3	9	6

Carriage Paid.

LEAN-TO PORTABLE KENNEL AND RUN.
No. 346

House, 4ft. by 3ft. 6in. Run, 4ft. by 6ft.

Cash Price	£5	0	0
Wood Back for Run,		22/6	extra.
Corrugated Iron round Run		5/-	extra.
Reversible Trough		5/-	

Carriage Paid.

CATALOGUE FREE:
Norfolk Iron Works, Norwich.

BRITISH TERRIERS.

British Terriers:

Their Breeding, Management, and Training for Show or Work . .

In Two Divisions:

Division I.—English and Welsh.
Division II.—Scotch and Irish.

Illustrated.

By J. MAXTEE

*(Author of " Popular Dog Keeping " ; Editor of " The Fox Terrier,"
" The Collie," " The Greyhound," &c.).*

LONDON :
L. UPCOTT GILL, Bazaar Buildings, DRURY LANE, W.C.
1909

PREFACE.

WHEN the idea was first conceived of dividing up our subject into " English and Welsh Terriers " and " Scotch and Irish Terriers," it was suggested that the two sections would also be most usefully combined under one cover. This, it was thought, would add to facility of reference where the busy man was concerned and at the same time enable the individual, even if he were only interested in one particular section, to have ready at hand some information upon those practical details of kennel management that invariably prove the stumbling-block to the novice dog-keeper, no matter what might be his ultimate object. Until now no cheap work embodying such information was accessible to the " million " interested in dog-keeping as distinguished from dog-fancying. The full scope of the work is set forth in the title-page, but should there be any additional specific point on which a reader is desirous of obtaining further information, I shall always be pleased to afford this through the medium of the correspondence columns of *The Bazaar*.

J. MAXTEE.

JUNE, 1909.

CONTENTS.

➤

Division I.

DIVISION II.

DIVISION I.

English and Welsh Terriers

English and Welsh Terriers.

THE AIREDALE.

The Breed in the Making.

NORTHERN dog-lovers will no doubt think it fitting that a county so long and so honourably associated with sport as Yorkshire has been should give birth to one of our most generally useful hardy Terriers—the Airedale. Even those who have watched the gradual evolution of the various breeds of dogs now before the public can scarcely realise that the largest and one of the most popular of our Terriers was absolutely unknown to the pioneers of dog shows, and that its history does not go back much more than half a century. Yet such is the fact. Undeniably difficult in the case of breeds generally is it to arrive at their *fons et origo*, and the Airedale Terrier is no exception to the rule. Though belonging to a comparatively recent period, it is astonishing how little of what may be termed reliable data is forthcoming. The fact is, the variety under consideration, like many another that preceded it, was required for a specific purpose—to assist in the hunting of the " mephitic otter," and it mattered little, we can well imagine, to its earlier admirers what were the constituent parts employed to produce such a dog, so long as the resultant animal was capable of performing its allotted task. Though primarily the dog

B

was wanted as an aid to Otter-hounds, yet it was also used against any of the larger vermin, and was a favourite dog with the miner long ere Fashion claimed it. That the dog we now know as the Airedale Terrier fulfilled the expectations of its early admirers there cannot be two opinions.

Yorkshire, with its rapid streams, whose banks gave shelter to many an otter, had, like numbers of other counties,

Mr. Holland Buckley's Airedale Terrier, Ch. Master Royal
(an International champion).

districts in which there was a strain of Terrier renowned alike for its gameness, hardiness, and water qualities. That much is very well known; while even the type of Terrier favoured is almost equally so. Apparently, this Terrier in the early days was a rough-and-tumble, hard-coated black-and-tan

or even black animal, going to scale at from 17lb. to 19lb.,
and it was employed, as already stated, as an assistant to
Otter-hounds of certain districts. That the jackets of those
early progenitors of the breed were water-resisting goes
without saying. What, therefore, was more reasonable than for those who admired the Otter-hound
of that day and its canine assistant to combine the
blood of the two in order to produce a bigger and more
determined Terrier-like product? And that is really what
happened, although it is very difficult at this lapse
of time to trace with accuracy the individual or individuals who first suggested the mingling of hound with Terrier
blood. That some such cross was resorted to, the general
conformation of the earlier specimens leaves no reasonable
room for doubt. There were the hound type of head and
large ears, and it was not until after a dash of Bull-
Terrier had been employed and much uphill work undertaken on the part of the breeders that anything like the
present-day type was produced.

A Breed of Many Names.

Having briefly referred to what may be termed the
" ancient history " of a comparatively modern breed, we
will now briefly glance at the Terrier as known to us in the
'seventies. First it may be stated that the breed is one that
has boasted many names, and we are unable to call to mind
any other variety so plentifully favoured in respect thereof.
So far as can be traced, the earliest names bestowed on this
hound-terrier in its newly-emerged days were the Broken-
Haired or Working, the Waterside, and the Bingley Terrier.
Still, none of these names seemed to meet the general approval
of the fancy as at that time constituted, and the subject
was very freely discussed in the columns of the *Country*,
the *Live Stock Journal*, &c. Mainly at the instigation of
the late Mr. Hugh Dalziel, the name now adopted received
acceptance, and since that time (1878) has stood for the

breed that had its origin in the valleys watered by the Aire and the Wharfe.

Nor must it be supposed that it has held its present name without challenge. As recently as 1902 an attempt was made to curtail it to " Airedale," on the score that the word " Terrier " applied to such a big dog was inappropriate. The suggested innovation found comparatively few supporters, and eventually died a natural death. It was not until 1886 that the Airedale Terrier was elevated to the dignity of a variety by the Kennel Club.

Qualities and Uses.

To the average man on the look-out for a house-dog that while not being big or bulky is sufficiently businesslike to command respect when used as a personal guard, the Airedale may be confidently recommended. Alike in disposition and gameness the dog is excellent, while at the same time it is more amenable to discipline under trying circumstances than is the somewhat headstrong Bedlington Terrier. Robust as to constitution, a first-class water-dog, and an all-round useful substitute, when properly trained, for a sporting field dog, the variety may be said to combine qualities rarely found in any other breed of the great group of Terriers. Yet another point in favour of the Airedale is the fact that it is one of the breeds that have been found to give excellent results when used as war-dogs. The worst that can be urged against the variety is that for the ordinary work of the Terrier proper it is, of course, far too big; while it is a dog that requires careful handling as a youngster, or it may prove too " soft " on the one hand or too " game " on the other.

Peculiarities of the Breed.

Practically every breed of Terrier may be said to possess some peculiarity or to require some special preparation to fit it for show. The Airedale Terrier certainly does. First, there is a very marked difference between the youngster and the adult—so marked in fact that the circumstance has often given rise to unfounded suspicions and to very unpleasant correspondence on the part of prospective purchasers of puppies. An Airedale Terrier when born and for some time afterwards is about as different from the adult animal as it well could be. Indeed, it must be confessed that the young puppy approximates very closely as regards coat-appearance to a Black-and-Tan Terrier. The more pronounced the tan markings in the eye vicinity and on the feet, and the darker the puppies generally, the greater the chance as a rule of a coat of the proper texture and quality being assumed by the dog when furnished. Still, with Airedales, as with all other dogs, there are naturally many disappointments that the breeder will encounter even with puppies that promise well : Nature is never hard-and-fast, and we have met with puppies which, after giving promise of having a good flat jacket, eventually were wavy-coated.

Show Preparation.

Very readily might a novice wishing to show Airedales imagine that all he had to do was to buy a winning dog and successes would follow as a natural consequence. Nothing could be farther from the truth. Coats, even when of the orthodox colour and texture, vary considerably in other respects, and some individuals will require less than half the show preparation that it is necessary to bestow on others. Each individual is practically a law unto itself. Taken generally, Airedale Terriers have to undergo many an unpleasant quarter of an hour at the hands of the trimmer, or the " ploater," as he is sometimes called, some month or six weeks prior to being required for show. Stripping perhaps would be the more correct term to employ in connection with this business, and the novice who attempts to show the majority of Airedale Terriers in Nature's garb will find himself rudely awakened when he gets his charges into the ring. It is no part of our work to instruct how to

trim, if indeed it were possible; but it is necessary to tell
the novice what he has to expect, so that he may not
be caught napping.   If he is wise he will join the
ranks of the fancy, and he will then gradually get
initiated into the mysteries of the trimmer's art.   In
the meantime should he possess a specimen that is good
enough to show, he would be well-advised to allow
one of the " professionals " to look after the dog and prepare it for the eventful day.   He must not expect to run
before he can walk, and that there is a good deal to be
learned, or rather unlearned, before becoming expert as a
fancier with any breed of Terrier, attendance at a few of the
more important shows at which the Airedale is liberally

Spratt's Trimming Comb.

catered for will soon convince the most sceptical.   Apart,
too, from the actual show preparation that even the best dogs
must needs undergo to stand a chance of a prize, there is
the minor operation of docking first to be performed on every
puppy born.   The regulation dock for an Airedale Terrier
is that about half the tail should be left.   The best time to
perform the operation is during the first week of the puppies'
lives.   The actual method of docking is referred to when
dealing with the Fox-Terrier.

To return to the coat.   Taken generally, there is no better
way of grooming a broken-haired Terrier like the one under
notice than by means of one of the slanting-bristle brushes
(as shown in the illustration), and sold by what may be
termed fanciers' providers.   A really good grooming with
this should be given once a day at least.   As regards the
removal of the old and shaggy coat, there is nothing better
than the trimming or stripping combs, of which the one

shown is a very good type. Still, the best of these are made on the adjustable principle (see illustration) and are readily set. The one shown is made by Taylor, of Bradford. Often a novice allows the puppy-coat and the old coat to

Slanting-Bristle Brush for Terrier.

remain on, to the certain detriment of the latter, to say nothing of the appearance of the dog. Apart, too, from combs and brushes, and occasionally other appliances, used, the finishing touches have to be put on these Terriers by means of finger and thumb dipped in resin, and the coat by such means is literally plucked out. Naturally a dog does not like the ordeal; but in the case of a show specimen he so often has to undergo it that the probability is that the familiarity breeds contempt for it. A man to make a clean job of the head, shoulders, and legs must have a good eye; otherwise the dog, instead of being improved by the process, will be absolutely spoiled. Then, too, the individual dog must be carefully studied, and anything that tends to intensify a fault must be minimised if possible. When a dog that grows a heavy coat is about to be prepared for show, it

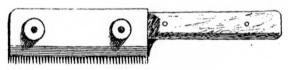

Taylor's Adjustable Trimming Comb.

is not wise to attempt too much in the way of plucking at one operation. Far better is it to make three, or even four, dressings at short intervals. As suggested above, no one can expect reasonably to be able to start straightaway and prepare one of these broken-haired Terriers for show. He must see the business carried through from start to finish several times before he is likely to make much of a hand at the business. And all this in face of the emphatic

rule of the Kennel Club against trimming! Without dressing, which is a mere euphemism for trimming, a dog has no
chance in the show-ring.

Popularity Abroad.

No sooner did this variety become popular here than
our American cousins, with that astuteness characteristic of
them, saw that it was one of the breeds likely to advance
still further in public favour, and forthwith set about purchasing some of our finest breeding-stock. Three-figure
sums for really good specimens were freely given, and for
a remarkably fine trio over £600 was paid to Mr. Mills.
This speaks volumes for a breed the best specimen of which
thirty years previously might have been obtained for a
modest " tenner " or a trifle more. Nor was it only in
America that the breed obtained a foothold, though it must
be confessed that in some of the more distant parts of the
globe—Japan, for instance—it was wanted rather for the
intelligence that it displayed and the readiness with which
it could be trained than for its good looks and typical
qualities. In France, Germany, and other European countries it found favour for a similar reason, and was more
than once one of the varieties selected as war-dogs. In our
Colonies, again, the breed has been very well represented,
and more than one excellent account of its gameness has
been sent home. Yet further employment has been found for
the breed, by France at any rate, for we hear of the Airedale
Terrier being selected to co-operate with the police in the
detection of crime—a part which it has since been called
upon to play in this country. It seems a little strange, however, that it should have been left to the representatives of
other nations to discover the utilitarian qualities of an
essentially British dog!

A Question of Size.

In the early 'nineties there was a danger, and a real one,
of this fine Terrier degenerating into a more or less diminu-

tive animal. At many of the more important shows small specimens were usurping the places of honour formerly held by the larger and more typical dog. In fact, much the same thing existed in the case of the Irish Terrier when there was an attempt to reduce the dog to the level of a red Fox-Terrier. However, in both cases the danger was averted. So far as the Airedale was concerned, the Club in its description (as will be seen) provided especially against the threatened danger, and size has been maintained and with it type. We have, however, heard one or two over-enthusiastic fanciers express a wish still further to increase the size of this Terrier; but we are unable to see what good purpose would be served thereby. To do so, alien—probably hound—blood would have to be employed, and as it was this that took the pioneers of the breed many long years of careful breeding to eliminate, the step would be retrogressive. We believe that in the States such a cross has been resorted to; but then that was done with a specific purpose and to suit a quarry that the dog was required to hunt. No such necessity exists here.

Selecting a Puppy.

How to select a puppy from the nest is one of those things which every novice wishes to know, but are so difficult to explain and calculated so often to prove disappointing. If a purchaser is wise he will wait until the puppies are six months old at least. By that time they will be showing more or less of their characteristics, and, allowing for the natural differences incidental to puppyhood, the purchaser should be able to select with practical certainty. If he has, say, the choice of several puppies returned from " walk " he should if possible select the one that combines the shortest back with the darkest eye, best placed (and smallest) ears and tail with the straightest and best boned legs, though such a happy combination is rarely found. Needless to say, a good mouth in a

Terrier is a *sine quâ non*, and the purchase of any puppy that has an overshot or an undershot mouth, or bad teeth, should not for one moment be entertained.

Description of the Breed.

The following is the description of the breed as drawn up by the Airedale Terrier Club :—

Head.—Long, with flat skull, not too broad between the ears and narrowing slightly to the eyes, free from wrinkle. Stop hardly visible, and cheeks free from fulness. Jaws deep and powerful, well filled up before the eyes; lips tight. Ears V-shaped, with a side carriage, small, but not out of proportion to the size of the dog. The nose is black. The eyes are small, and dark in colour, not prominent, but full of Terrier expression. The teeth are strong and level.

Neck.—Should be of moderate length and thickness, gradually widening towards the shoulders and free from throatiness.

Shoulders and Chest.—Shoulders long, and sloping well into the back; shoulder-blades flat. Chest deep, but not broad.

Body.—Back short, strong, and straight. Ribs well sprung.

Hindquarters.—Strong and muscular, with no droop. Hocks well let down. The tail is set on high, and carried gaily.

Legs and Feet.—Legs perfectly straight, with plenty of bone. Feet small and round, with a good depth of pad.

Coat.—Hard and wiry, and not so long as to appear ragged; it should also be straight and close, covering the dog well all over the body and legs.

Colour.—The head and ears, with the exception of dark markings on each side of the skull, should be tan, the ears being of a darker shade than the rest. The legs up to the thighs and elbows are also tan. The body is black or dark grizzle.

Size.—Dogs, 40lb. to 45lb.; bitches slightly less.

It is the unanimous opinion of the Club that the size of the Airedale Terrier as given in the above standard is one of, if not the most important characteristic of the breed. All judges who shall henceforth adjudicate on the merits of the Airedale Terrier shall consider under-sized specimens of the breed severely handicapped when competing with dogs of the standard weight. And that any of the Club's judges who, in the opinion of the Committee, shall give prizes or otherwise push to the front dogs of a small type, shall be at once struck off from the list of specialist judges.

THE BEDLINGTON.

Early History.

JUST as the district in the near vicinity of the Aire and the Wharfe may be said to have produced our largest and one of our smartest Terriers, so we must allocate the origin of the fastest Terrier to the country adjacent to the Coquet and the Tyne. Though to the mining village of Bedlington the dog owes the name it bears, yet such, it may be taken, was merely complimentary, and probably largely due to the fact that it was kept more numerously there than in any other district. It might with equal correctness have been dubbed the Rothbury Terrier. From the very nature of the men largely constituting the inhabitants of .that centre one can very well surmise the kind of dog that would appeal to them. Game it would have to be, and not only capable of holding its own when pitted against others of its kind, but fast enough to catch a rabbit in the open, sporting enough to tackle anything from fox to badger, a first-rate water dog, and withal a desirable companion. All this, apparently, the early Bedlington Terriers were, if we may rely upon the historians of a century and more ago. In fact, even after this lapse of time, when the dog has been bred for show rather than for serious work, it maintains the majority of its old characteristics.

Some years ago in the columns of the *Field* there was discussed in an excellent and informing contribution the early history of this distinctive Terrier; and nothing so authoritative had ever before, nor has since, appeared with regard thereto. In that the origin of the breed as a breed could be traced no farther back than the first quarter of the nineteenth century. No doubt, as in the case of many other varieties, there existed locally a game Terrier that was kept more par-

ticularly by the nomadic tinkers, gipsies, &c., who travelled
the country in search of work—and sport! These dogs were
used to furnish sport for poor man and rich man alike, being
often employed as assistants to hounds. If we rely upon
the contribution already referred to, we must take as the
starting-point of the breed the mating of the two kennel
Terriers owned by Mr. E. Donkin, the Master of the

**A Typical Present-day Type of Bedlington Terrier.—Mr. Harold
Warne's strain.**

Flotterton Hounds. We may take it that these early
progenitors of the breed were very closely related to
the Dandie Dinmont Terriers on the other side of
the Border ; it does not require any stretch of the
imagination to see that the two varieties, even now,
have much in common. However this may be, the
actual honour of mating the two said kennel Terriers rests
with Joseph Ainsley, a working man, who was afterwards
identified still more closely with the variety. There are
enthusiastic admirers of this Terrier who would claim for

it an unbroken descent of a century and a quarter ; but there is nothing tangible to be adduced in support of this, and we are inclined rather to rely upon the *Field* contribution referred to for the real facts of the case.

Distinctive Features.

Although there are certain outward characteristics in the Bedlington Terrier that point unmistakably to its relationship with the Dandie Dinmont Terrier, yet there are wide divergences. The Bedlington alike as regards build and colour stands practically alone. It is well described as a " lathy " dog, and the lines on which it is built at once show that it is speedy—the speediest, in fact, of all the Terriers. Like its first cousin, the Dandie, its head is crowned with a topknot of a lighter colour than that of the hair on the body, and it is this which has often proved the undoing of the exhibitor who prefers to produce artificially rather than naturally topknots of the requisite shade. Then, again, the ears are filbert-shaped—giving the Terrier a quaint appearance. To look at the Bedlington Terrier as he appears in the show-ring, the dog will be seen to have an extraordinarily lamb-like head when viewed casually and from a certain point. Such an expression certainly belies his courage and is calculated to deceive a novice in search of a really game and all-round sporting Terrier. The topknot has to be encouraged and emphasised in every way, and this point must be remembered when preparing these dogs for show.

Qualities, Temperament, and Constitution.

Allusion has already been made to the many ways in which the Bedlington Terrier has been employed in sport, and just a passing mention has been made of his companionable qualities. The latter, however, deserve to be widely known. That the Terrier under discussion is a trifle headstrong may be true, more especially where little care has been bestowed upon its upbringing ; but this we regard as the fault of the owners rather than of the dogs. A somewhat jealous disposition combined with a very game nature is now and again responsible for a kennel fight in cases where there has been neglect to remove some tit-bit carried inside. Still, it should not be deduced from such slender data that the breed is quarrelsome. Properly brought up this sensible variety is as well-behaved as any other member of the Terrier group. That the dog will fight when provoked—what Terrier worth its keep will not ?—and punish most severely is certainly true; but that is the worst that can be said against it. Frequently it is said that the variety generally is a capricious feeder, and requires more than ordinary care. This may be taken, as applied to the breed generally, as erroneous, though there are, of course, individuals that may be classed as " bad doers," as there are in every breed of Domestic dog.

In constitution the dog is hardy by nature; but owing no doubt to the large amount of in-breeding that has been resorted to for the purpose of fixity of type, there are strains that show enfeebled vitality, and this is chiefly seen in the puppies in the earlier stages of their existence. The long-head craze has probably been a factor that has worked injuriously for the breed : for it is impossible unduly to exaggerate any point without some other suffering and the symmetry of the animal being thereby lost. Happily this craze shows signs of abatement, and a more equally-balanced Terrier is the result.

Still with all the recommendations that the Bedlington Terrier has, it is not, nor has it ever been, a popular breed. In fact, it would be correct to say that in the southern half of England the variety is scarcely known, the more's the pity.

Old v. Present-day Type.

A good deal might be said under this head with reference to the future well-being of the breed. Compared with the type of dog that existed thirty years or so ago, the modern counterpart loses considerably. There are, of course, individuals nowadays that are quite equal to any that we can call to mind in the palmiest days of the variety; but as a whole the breed has suffered by losing some of its more notable characteristics. As with many other Terriers, the Bedlington is one that has suffered from the extra-long-head craze, and we see the reflex of this in the less rounded character of the head in the vicinity of the occiput. Coats, it will, we think, be generally admitted, are nothing like so good in texture or in colour, the former being soft and the latter light. Such coats as are found in many a modern representative of the breed would stand the individuals in little stead were they called upon to work very much in water or in the wet. Similarly, one notices far too many undershot and overshot mouths in a breed in which a level mouth is supposed to be a characteristic, and far too many light-eyed dogs. If judges were oftener to examine the mouths of Terriers generally, a state of affairs would be revealed that would surprise them. There is not the slightest reason why the present-day Bedlington Terrier should not be improved as regards the characteristics referred to; and if this were done, the excellent qualities of the Terrier made better known, and the "hairdressing" inseparable from the breed as it exists at present done away with, there would, we think, be a big future for this essentially North-country Terrier.

As a Show Dog.

Nearly forty years have elapsed since the Bedlington first appeared in the show-ring, and it must be confessed that it is an entirely different-looking dog now from what it was then. At that time "trimming" was not resorted to, and the dog was shown more as Nature intended than as man thought fit. Grooming it had in plenty; but that was all. To many of those who know the present-day dog it would be a revelation to see prints of this old-time Terrier. It is this trimming that has proved so injurious to the breed; for not only has it prevented progress being made, but it has

deterred many who otherwise admire the dog from taking it
up.   There are plenty of men who object to the wholesale
trimming that such breeds have to undergo and the constant
plucking necessary to fit them for show if they are to stand
any chance.   Nor is this trimming an art readily learned and
practised ; consequently dogs that are to be prepared have
often to be submitted to one of the professional " hair-
dressers " for treatment.   The long coat is stripped from the
body ; while the face, muzzle, and tail have to be plucked
in order to give the dog the artificial appearance that present-
day judges stickle for.   Not content with such barbering,
there are men who go a step further and artificially lighten
the topknot.   When purchasing one of these dogs it is therefore advisable to pass a dark handkerchief over or otherwise
carefully to examine the silky topknot for evidences of a more
permanent colouring matter being used in the form of stain.
As compared with the old-time dogs many show-bred
specimens are leggier, lighter in eye, more roach-backed, far
too soft and light as to coat, and bigger ; while the lamb-
like look that the trimmed head gives is suggestive of anything but the determination that the breed in the past was
noted for.

As regards the length of coat favoured, the most prominent breeders pronounce for an inch jacket as far as the body
is concerned.   Now there is not a Bedlington Terrier bred
to the adult stage that would grow such a jacket even though
it may be groomed (as ordinarily understood) day in day out.
Moreover, such a jacket as we see on the Bedlington would
not be of the slightest protection to a dog subjected to
much exposure, to say nothing of one that was required
to " water," as it was before these latter-day enthusiasts
thought fit to " hairdress " it contrary to Nature's
laws.   All sorts of devices are employed by " trimmers " to
pull out not only the old coat but the fast coat as well.
Special combs of wonderful construction are advertised by
many ; while other devices such as resin are employed in the
" plucking " of Terriers generally.   The farce of the

business is that "trimming" as practised is theoretically
prohibited; actually it is allowed. The fancier who loves
the Bedlington for its fearless courage and many endearing
qualities and wishes to show must either "trim" his dogs
or, better still, as already suggested, get some past-master in
the art to do so, or for ever give up the idea of meeting the
experienced men on equal terms.

Years ago the fashionable colour was liver : to-day it is
blue, or what passes for that colour ; and in this connection
it may not be out of place to refer to the fact that the two
colours are occasionally crossed, with advantage so long as
it is done judiciously. Blue is a more taking colour than the
others allowed ; but on the principle that a good dog, like a
good horse, cannot be of a bad colour, there are to be found
in both colours animals worthy of the best traditions of the
breed.

As with the Dandie Dinmont Terrier, the topknot is not
produced until the adult stage is reached; therefore in
selecting a young puppy one has to take not a little chance.
Still, a domed skull it must have, good straight legs, flat
ribs, and a level mouth. The last-named is a most essential
point in any Terrier, and in the Bedlington it is one that
is not as often taken into consideration as its importance
warrants.

Description.

No lack of specialist clubs exists with a view to upholding
the standard of the breed, and the description that follows
is the one drawn up by the National Bedlington Terrier
Club :—

Skull.—Narrow, but deep and rounded; high at occiput, and
covered with a nice silky tuft or topknot.

Jaw.—Long, tapering, sharp, and muscular ; as little stop as
possible between the eyes, so as to form nearly a line from the nose-
end along the joint of the skull to the occiput. The lips close-
fitting, and no flew.

Eyes.—Should be small and well sunk into the head. The blues

                                                        c

should have a dark eye; the blue-and-tan ditto, with amber shade; livers, sandies, &c., a light brown eye.

Nose.—Large, well angled. Blues and blue-and-tans should have black noses; livers and sandies flesh-coloured noses.

Teeth.—Level, or pincer-jawed.

Ears.—Moderately large, carried well forward, flat to the cheek, thinly covered, and tipped with fine silky hair; they should be filbert-shaped.

Legs.—Of moderate length, not wide apart, straight and square set and with good-sized feet, which are rather long.

Tail.—Thick at root, tapering to a point, slightly feathered on lower side, 9in. to 11in. long, and scimitar-shaped.

Neck and Shoulders.—Neck long, deep at base, rising well from shoulders, which should be flat.

Body.—Long and well-proportioned, flat ribbed and deep; not wide in chest; back slightly arched, well ribbed up, with light quarters.

Coat.—Hard, with close bottom, and not lying flat to the sides.

Colour.—Dark blue, blue and tan, liver, liver and tan, sandy, sandy and tan.

Height.—About 15in. to 16in.

General Appearance.—A lightly made-up, lathy dog, but not shelly.

Weight.—Dogs, about 24lb.; bitches, about 22lb.

THE BLACK-AND-TAN TERRIER.

Rise and Fall of the Breed.

FROM very early times a black-and-tan dog of Terrier type
has been in evidence; but whether or not this is the progenitor of the breed we now regard as the Black-and-Tan or
Manchester Terrier is more than can be stated authorita-
tively. All that can be said with any certainty is that
appearances point that way, and that, at any rate from the
earliest days of the nineteenth century, if not before, there
has been, according to Daniel, the author of "Rural Sports,"
" an elegant black-and-tan, sprightly smooth-coated Terrier."
Still, with a perversity that is characteristic of the old writers
upon dogs, there is none of the descending to finer details
that the present-day historian would so much value and that
would help those interested in different breeds to deduce
therefrom some practical facts. However, we may assume
with a fair measure of accuracy that the old type of
dog was much coarser than its modern counterpart, and
thereby better qualified for the work of the rat-pit in particular and of a vermin-killer in general. Doubtless its more
refined appearance dates from the period when shows became
a power and thus gave an incentive to breeders to produce a
smarter-looking animal.

Many conjectures have been rife as to the constituents
used in the making of the Black-and-Tan Terrier of to-day,
and the suggestion of the introduction of Whippet blood
seems a perfectly reasonable one. Be that as it may, the Black-
and-Tan Terrier was in its zenith a little short of half a
century ago, though it did not attain perfection of markings
until the 'sixties, when Mr. Sam Handley came upon the scene.
Its decadent period, on the other hand, dates from the time
the edict went forth to abolish the cruel practice of cropping

—namely, in 1895. From that time onward the breed has gone from bad to worse.

Besides the abolition of cropping already alluded to there were other factors that contributed to the downfall of this smart Terrier. These were the malpractices that existed in connection with the show-dog. At one time it was no uncommon thing for a badly-marked specimen to be " painted up " in such a way as almost to defy detection, and there existed men who were considered experts at the business of

Type of Black-and-Tan Terrier.—Mr. Higgs's strain.

providing the much-coveted toe-pencillings. It was the notorious faking, combined with the cropping edict, the difficulty experienced in breeding good specimens, and the advent of other breeds, that put the noses of the Black-and-Tan Terriers out of joint. Much as one admires the lines on which a good specimen is built, the only conclusion that can be arrived at is that unless something unforeseen happens the Black-and-Tan Terrier's circle of followers will be still more restricted in the future. Even around Manchester and other Lancashire districts the dog is not by any means plentiful ; while in the South and West its coterie of admirers is

smaller, and we still look for dogs of the type that Mr.
W. K. Taunton, Mr. Littler, Mr. H. Lacy, Mr. James
Hinks, Rev. W. J. Meller, Mr. Parry, and many another
used to have.

The Prefix "Manchester."

Nowadays, though it is the custom to ignore the old
prefix of Manchester as applied to this Terrier, yet there
is no valid reason why such an appropriate name should
be entirely lost sight of. There can be no doubt that
Manchester and its environs in the early 'sixties, when the
breed was in the zenith of its popularity, furnished the
great majority of the specimens that one met with at shows
and elsewhere, and it was on this account that the prefix
Manchester came to be associated with the breed and even
to be recognised by the Kennel Club itself. We are somewhat conservative as to these old names, and would have
them preserved as far as possible, more especially when,
as in this case, the name is fittingly applied.   To
this day, moreover, there are quite a number of fanciers
who prefer the term Manchester to that of Black-and-
Tan Terrier, and therefore it would seem only fair to
use Manchester, if not as a varietal name, at least as
a synonym.   We have already referred to one of the
principal Manchester fanciers associated with the breed in
Mr. Sam Handley, and probably no contemporary of his
had so many of these Terriers pass through his hands. Of
the Southerners alive at the present time who played any
important part in fashioning the breed and bringing it to
its high state of perfection, we can only call to mind
one—Mr. W. K. Taunton, who for years acted as Hon.
Secretary to the Black-and-Tan Terrier Club. His earliest
connection with the breed dates back to about 1865, some
nine years ere he espoused the cause of the Mastiff.

Claims as Worker and House Dog.

Whatever claims the coarser Black-and-Tan Terrier may
have had to be considered a game working dog, it would

scarcely be correct to say that such a characteristic has been transmitted to its smarter relative. More than a score of years ago we had a nice-looking descendant of Champion Wallace that would kill rats with almost any dog against which it was pitted; yet we had but to allow the dog to come in the vicinity of a stoat or a weasel for it to be thoroughly scared. On the other hand, a better dog for the house hardly exists, and it is in this capacity rather than as a dog for the man of sporting tendencies that this Terrier may be recommended. It has no coat to show dirt, and on this account it might be kept in manufacturing and other centres in which a white or other light-coated breed would be unsuited. Again, it is a breed that will thrive upon a minimum of exercise as compared with Terriers generally, so long as it is carefully fed. It cannot be regarded as a delicate breed; but it is one that is best kept running about the house.

Show Preparation.

Being a very symmetrical Terrier, built on somewhat fine lines, the breed under notice must not be shown fat, otherwise its graceful proportions will be destroyed. As regards actual preparation, though the touching-up in respect of the breed is not so difficult as in the case of the broken-haired varieties, yet it must not be supposed that the very smart appearance is altogether Nature's handiwork. The tail in particular comes in for its share of preparation by a process known as "fining." Here again the practice is declared illegal, yet the feathering beneath the tail is often removed in spite of such a declaration. The glossy coat one so much admires is obtained by plenty of good grooming—using a hound glove—hand-rubbing with just a little oil in the palm, though every trace of it must be removed prior to the dog's facing the judge. Then feeding is an important factor in the production of a nice glossy jacket. A little boiled fish now and then is calculated to produce a gloss, as is a little linseed oil given at intervals of a fortnight or less in the soft food or even alone. Some fanciers aver that the wearing of clothing improves the coat texture.

Buying a Show Dog.

There has been in the past so much swindling in connection with this breed that it behoves the young hand to be careful, especially when purchasing in the open market. Toe-pencillings, thumb-marks, and other desirable characteristics may be produced by the aid of paint and pencil, just as the requisite shade of deep tan may be produced by certain dyes; while undesirable white hairs on chest may be disguised by a similar agency, or, for the time being, removed by plucking. So far as the last-named is concerned, it may be said that it is impossible to remove the roots, and therefore if the dog be carefully examined by the aid of a glass the base of any such white hairs would show. One should be especially careful when buying a very young dog, in which the coveted markings would not appear naturally. Still, no breeder of repute would descend to such trickery. In this connection it may be as well to state that in litters one occasionally finds a blue-and-tan whelp. This is by no means to be despised for breeding purposes.

Description.

The following is a description of the breed as drawn up by the Black-and-Tan Terrier Club :—

Head.—Long, flat, and narrow, level and wedge-shaped, without showing cheek muscles; well filled up under the eyes, with tapering, tightly lipped jaws and level teeth.

Eyes.—Very small, sparkling, and dark, set fairly close together, and oblong in shape.

Nose.—Black.

Ears.—Small, V-shaped, and dropped; set as close together as possible at the top of the head.

Neck and Shoulders.—The neck should be fairly long, and tapering from the shoulders to the head, with sloping shoulders, the neck being free from throatiness, and slightly arched at the junction with the occiput.

Chest.—Narrow but deep.

Body.—Moderately short and curving upwards at the loin; ribs well sprung, back slightly arched at the loin and falling again at the joining of the tail to the same height as the shoulders.

Legs.—Must be quite straight, set on well under the dog, and of fair length.

Feet.—More inclined to be cat- than hare-footed.

Tail.—Moderate length, and set on where the arch of the back ends; thick where it joins the body, tapering to a point, and not carried higher than the back.

Coat.—Close, smooth, short, and glossy.

Colour.—Jet black and rich mahogany tan, distributed over the body as follows : On the head the muzzle is tanned to the nose, which, with the nasal bone, is jet black; there is also a bright spot on each cheek, and above each eye, the under jaw and throat are tanned, and the hair *inside* the ear is of the same colour; the fore legs tanned up to the knee, with black lines (pencil marks) up each toe, and a black mark (thumb mark) above the foot; *inside* the hind legs tanned, but divided with black at the hock joint; and under the tail also tanned; and so is the vent, but only sufficiently to be easily covered by the tail; also slightly tanned on each side of chest. Tan on the *outside* of the hind legs— commonly called breeching—is a serious defect. In all cases the black should not run into the tan, or *vice versâ,* but the division between the two colours should be well defined.

General Appearance.—A Terrier, calculated to take his own part in the rat-pit, and not of the Whippet type.

Weight.—From 16lb. to 20lb. is most desirable.

STANDARD OF POINTS.

Head	20
Eyes	10
Ears	5
Legs	10
Feet	10
Body	10
Tail	5
Colour and Markings	15
General Appearance	15
Total	100

THE BORDER TERRIER.

A Rare Variety.

THE Border Terrier is as yet comparatively unknown.
Its name at once proclaims its origin. Needless to
say, like its near relatives the Dandie Dinmont and
the Bedlington Terrier, it is noted for its hard-bitten
nature and gameness. Here, again, we have a dog required
for a special purpose and adapted, moreover, for work
under most difficult conditions. Anyone conversant with
the peat-moss holes of the Border counties—runners of
water found at the bottom of the mosses and frequently
extending several hundred yards—will at once appreciate
this; but the Southerner who is familiar with fox-hunting
as it is carried out in his part of the country cannot even
faintly imagine what it means to conduct the sport under
the conditions obtaining in the districts in the North that
have produced this very excellent Terrier. The breed,
which for a generation has been bred for work, has never
deteriorated, and to-day is as game as it was in the days
of Ned Dunn, of Whitelee, Reedwater, and Yeddie Jack-
son, both of whom were renowned for possessing a strain
of these game Terriers. Occasionally one sees it at shows in
the Border counties, but there it is judged by no artificial
standard, and the result is that while an essentially working
breed like the Dandie Dinmont, produced almost in the
same locality, has degenerated into nothing more than a
fashionable beauty, the Border Terrier is the exact antithesis
and is as sturdy as the Northern yeomen who often keep it
for the sport it affords. To followers of the Border Fox-
hounds the Terrier is, of course, best known, while there
are families like the Dodds, the Robsons, the Elliotts,

the Hedleys, &c., with which it has been identified for generations.

Description.

A Terrier whose mission in life is to work against foxes found not in earths of the generally accepted type, but in those situated in rocky fastnesses, and to travel underground in the cold moss-runners referred to, must naturally possess

Types of Border Terriers.—Mr. Dodd's strain.

characteristics that will enable it to do so. No Terrier with a poor nose, a poor coat, or deficient in courage would be of use, any more than would one deficient in stamina. In weight this Terrier would scale from 14lb. to 18lb.; while an average shoulder height would be 14in. The coat colour varies considerably, from the red of an Irish Terrier, grey-brindled, dark blue body with tan legs, to black and tan. The nature of the coat also differs, for whereas some are smooth, others are broken-haired, the former being more in request. The head partakes of that of the Fox-Terrier, but is neither so long nor so strong; while the ears, instead of being carried close to the head, are half-pricked. Unlike the majority of Terriers, the one under notice is not docked.

Good Types.

The illustration shows two typical Border Terriers—dogs, moreover, that in their time distinguished themselves as fox-bolters. Both were owned by Mr. G. T. Dodd, and were about as keen as mustard. They were at home with any kind of vermin, and, as is the case with the variety generally, were sensible to a degree. The dog (on the right) combined excellent working qualities with a good appearance, and was many times a winner in the show-ring. Like many another game specimen of the breed, however, he came to an untimely end, probably in one of the fox-earths to which allusion has been made. The bitch (on the left), on account of her maternal duties, had not the same opportunities to show her skill as the dog, but her owner nevertheless stated that whenever tried she was not found wanting.

THE BULL-TERRIER.

A Dog with a "Past."

IF we except, perhaps, the Bulldog, one of the chief constituents used in the production of the Bull-Terrier, no variety of the domestic dog has been so unjustly libelled as the one under notice. It has often been used as a text by the moralists who wished to preach a sermon exemplifying that a man may be judged by the variety of dog that he keeps. In fact, if some of these gentry could have had their way the Bull-Terrier would long ere this have ceased to be. That the Bull-Terrier as it was originally known suffered somewhat from the age in which it was evolved admits of little doubt; but it was the then owners rather than the dogs that should have been condemned. From the earliest times of which we have any record of man and dog existing as it were side by side, there have been fighting dogs and fighting men; but if we are to believe some of these preachers, it was not until the advent of the Bull-Terrier that there was a fighting dog.

Origin of the Breed.

Anyone but casually acquainted with the breed would say at once that the very name indicated its origin—namely, a compound of Bulldog and Terrier. This, however, is only partially correct. Something more than these elements was required to build up the framework of the big dog that we know to-day, scaling anything up to nearly 50lb., and it is therefore reasonable to assume that the Mastiff (the Bull-Mastiff is a common enough dog), Pointer, and Dalmatian also contributed their quota; while some breeders go so far as to say that both Whippet and Greyhound also were used. Be this as it may, in some of the smaller Bull-Terriers one finds traces of Whippet characteristics. There is nothing authoritative to point the way with certainty to the variety of Terrier originally employed to cross with

Bull-Terrier of the famous Bloomsbury strain.

the Bulldog, though from a knowledge of the Bull-Terrier as it was forty years or so ago, it would seem to be the Black-and-Tan Terrier. Then followed perhaps some such crosses as were suggested above, giving us the brindle, pied, liver, and other coloured Bull-Terriers that were well known for their fighting qualities; and eventually Mr. James Hinks,

of Birmingham, further experimented with the English White
Terrier, and ended by giving us the milk-white dog that is
recognised to-day.   Still, many years after the introduction
of this white dog it was not unusual to have patched dogs
turning up in litters, and even in the show-ring.   In the
early days, too, of the white dog there were very typical
medium-sized dogs—16lb. to 25lb.—but these now are
practically non-existent, the heavy-weights having quite
usurped the position formerly held by the middle-weights.

The Boston Terrier.

In the United States there is a most popular dog in the
Boston Terrier, an offshoot of the Bull-Terrier and the
Bulldog.   It reminds one forcibly of the latter as depicted in
early eighteenth-century prints.   There is nothing suggestive
of the modern Bull-Terrier in its appearance, the skull being
round rather than flat.   It is a cropped dog of from 12lb.
to about 30lb. in weight, is preferred of a brindle colour,
and has a considerable amount of white about it, even to
the feet.

The Abolition of Cropping.

For many years the show Bull-Terrier was subjected to
the very cruel operation of ear-cropping ; indeed, it was
not until 1895 the edict went forth (after a conviction)
abolishing it.   Many prophesied, and with more or less truth,
that this would mean the practical extinction of the breed.
That for a time it worked prejudicially against a dog never
by any stretch of the imagination to be regarded as a popular
one is certainly true, and for several years the breed
has passed through troublous days.   So long had the
admirers become accustomed to the erect, cropped, well-
shaven ear, giving to the head a determined expression, that
the " softening " (refining) effect the natural ear gave was
not liked.   Even now the great ear question—that is, its
shape—has not been finally settled, though the rose ear, as

seen on the Bulldog and several other breeds, would seem to be the most suitable. The Terrier ear detracts considerably from the expression, and is scarcely likely to be the vogue ; while the semi-erect ear has not many followers. To-day the breed is in far better favour than for many years, and it only needs for those acting in its best interests to remove the unjust and erroneous impressions with regard to it for the dog to become really popular.

True Character and Uses.

From a knowledge of the Bull-Terrier extending well back into the 'sixties, a knowledge, moreover, gained by keeping and breeding it, and watching narrowly its behaviour under differing circumstances, we can say that as a companion and personal guard there is no dog its size that can equal it when really well-trained. The savage and bloodthirsty character with which many credit it may be dismissed as moonshine—if only the dog be rationally treated. That it is a strong, game, and determined Terrier, with a jaw-power second to none, anyone who has kept the dog will know ; but it is possible for a dog to have these and yet for it to be as well-mannered as the most meek and mild Toy that was ever born. With children its behaviour is ideal, and no breed that we can call to mind will stand so much pulling about from youngsters. There are, however, two things that the prospective owner should guard against— a mongrel, that by courtesy only may be considered a Bull-Terrier, and a chained-up specimen. A pure-bred Bull-Terrier, taken generally, is reliable in every way ; but cross it with almost any other breed possible, and the resulting product will be anything but " sweet " in temperament, and especially when treated as if it were incapable of appreciating freedom and association with man.

Often sportsmen journeying to hot countries are anxious to learn of a dog that, while being game enough to be entered to certain small " game," is at the same time likely to be able to withstand the climate. To such the Bull-Terrier may be recommended, for long ago its worth was proved in India, Africa, and elsewhere. Carrying but a scanty coat, the dog does not feel the extreme heat like a long-coated breed does, and on that account makes a most desirable " pal " to anyone obliged to live in such countries.

Elsewhere we have hinted at the uses, or rather mis-uses, to which this game dog was put in the 'fifties and the 'sixties. For fighting, for the rat-pit, and also for assisting in the not very edifying sport of badger-baiting, the Bull-Terrier was much in demand. All this has been changed, and to-day the variety is one of the most com-panionable and even-tempered of all the Terriers.

Being mostly pure white, Bull-Terriers soon soil their coats if kept in crowded, smoky towns, necessitating constant washing or dry-cleaning if they are to look presentable. For all that, they are dogs which seem to thrive on com-paratively little exercise, and on that account alone would be considered desirable by those who have neither the time nor the inclination to devote themselves to the exercising of one of the very active breeds.

There is scarcely any need to say that the Bull-Terrier makes an ideal vermin-dog, though it may not be so well known that it may readily be trained to take to the water. Still, by reason of its scanty coat it cannot stand weather like its broken-haired relatives.

If it is wished to make a Bull-Terrier a good guard, it should be fed, exercised, groomed, and generally tended by the owner or some member of the household. We may, however, state in this connection that a dog of any breed is best kept *indoors* at night and allowed the run of the house, once good manners have been inculcated. Instinctively the dog will assume the rôle of protector over such an individual. Care must be taken with all white dogs to find out if they are sound of hearing.   In the past many Bull-Terriers were deaf, and even nowadays the defect occasionally crops up.

Puppy-Rearing Hints.

Bull-Terrier bitches have large litters, and make ideal mothers. No bitch should, however, be called upon to rear more than five. For the rest a " foster " should be provided. The puppies, when they are of any size, should not be kept too many together or a battle-royal is sure to take place, with probably dire results. Being big-boned, big-framed dogs, it is customary among experienced breeders not only to provide bone-forming foods, but also to give with soft food a little bone-meal or phosphate of calcium sprinkled thereon. Plenty of fresh air and sunshine, combined with judicious exercise, are necessary to the making of a healthy adult.

Show Preparation.

The treatment suggested for English White Terriers will apply in the main to this Terrier, though, being a far more muscular dog, plenty of good, fairly fast walking exercise, with vigorous hand-rubbing, will tend to the desired end.

Description.

The following description of the Bull-Terrier was drawn up by the Bull-Terrier Club :—

General Appearance.—The general appearance of the Bull-Terrier is that of a symmetrical animal, and the embodiment of agility, grace, elegance, and determination.

Head.—The head should be long, flat, and wide between the ears, tapering to the nose, without cheek-muscles. There should be a slight indentation down the face, without a " stop " between the eyes. The jaws should be long and very powerful, with a large black nose and open nostrils. The eyes should be small and very black, almond shape preferred. The lips should meet as tightly as possible, without a fold. The teeth should be regular in shape and should meet exactly; any deviation, such as pig-jaw, or being under-hung, is a great fault.

Neck.—The neck should be long and slightly arched, nicely set into the shoulders, tapering to the head without any loose skin, as found in the Bulldog.

D

Shoulders.—The shoulders should be strong, muscular, and slanting ; the chest wide and deep, with ribs well rounded.

Back.—This should be short and muscular, but not out of proportion to the general contour of the animal.

Legs.—The fore legs should be perfectly straight, with well-developed muscles; not out "at shoulder," but set on the racing lines, and very strong at the pastern joints. The hind legs should be long, and, in proportion to the fore legs, muscular, with good, strong, straight hocks, well let down near the ground.

Feet.—These should resemble more closely those of a cat than a hare.

Colour.—Should be white.

Coat.—Short, close, and stiff to the touch, with a fine gloss.

Tail.—This should be short in proportion to the size of the dog, set on very low down, thick where it joins the body, and tapering. It should be carried at an angle of about 45 degrees, without curl, and never over the back.

Weight.—From 15lb. to 50lb.

Toy Bull-Terriers.

Though many attempts have been made to produce a Toy Bull-Terrier, yet the measure of success so far attained has been insignificant. Comparatively few specimens can be called to mind during the last thirty years that can truly be said to have been small editions of the larger dog. The least satisfactory have been the very small ones from which the apple-round head seems inseparable · while tail-carriage generally in such dogs leaves a deal to be desired. That a dog of from 3lb. to 10lb. the counterpart of the larger Bull-Terrier would appeal to numbers of dog fanciers is certain. It now rests with breeders to produce one.

From 4lb. to 8lb. or 10lb. would seem to be the range of weight of these Toy Bull-Terriers, which, contrary to the generally-entertained opinion, are dogs that have been known and bred at least from the time of the last George. At one time, before the advent of so many more engaging-looking Toy dogs from other climes, the miniature Bull-Terrier certainly had something of a vogue in fashionable circles, though nothing like that of the Toy Spaniels, one variety of which was a favourite with the " Merry Monarch."

Despite its comparatively small size, the Toy Bull-Terrier of old was, like its larger relative, very courageous, and was often used in the rat-pit. Similarly, too, it resembled the larger dog in that it was not, as now, of a milk-white colour. Brindled markings were common enough, as were also other colours associated with the larger animal, and even with the Bulldog, which played no inconsiderable part in its making. There are few breeders of these miniatures now, though Lord and Lady Decies occasionally show some nice specimens.

Elsewhere reference has been made to two or three of the more glaring faults of this little dog. Yet another is the crooked legs that one almost always finds. When we come to think of the constituents from which Bull-Terriers were evolved it is, of course, not difficult to account for such defects. Oftener than not, these miniatures approximate far more closely to English White Terriers than to Bull-Terriers, and no acknowledged standard of type by which to breed has yet been published.

THE ENGLISH WHITE TERRIER.

A Decadent Breed.

UNDENIABLY smart as this neatly-made Terrier is, yet it is
not one on which Fashion has set her seal, and it has
suffered accordingly. Indeed, it may be written down as a
decadent breed, and however much one may admire it as
a house-dog and companion, it has little or no following,
save, perhaps, a small one in the North and in Scotland.
Its unpopularity is, perhaps, best indicated by show classifi-
cations, in which it nowadays seldom figures. Even at
such representative gatherings as the Kennel Club, Birmingham, and Cruft's it is not thought worth while to cater
for it, and, unless the breed receives a very decided fillip, it
looks as if it will ere long have to be reckoned as a
Terrier of the past. That this is so is to be
deplored, for it possesses certain characteristics that
should commend themselves to Terrier lovers, fashioned
as it is on the lines of the better-known Black-
and-Tan or Manchester Terrier. Years ago, in the early
days of dog shows, it had not a few admirers, but the
abolition of cropping seemed to seal its doom. Anyhow,
from that time to the present it has been gradually going
down hill, despite the efforts of a few enthusiasts to revive
an interest in it.

In the old days the English White Terrier, like its near
relative the Bull-Terrier, had to endure a very unpleasant
time at the hands of the skilful hairdresser, apart from
the brutal cropping operation that it was necessary for
every show specimen to undergo. Not content with removing
a portion of the ears, these latter had to be shaved clean,
while the other extremity—the tail—had to be trimmed

and fined in various ways, according to the dictates of the particular individual responsible for the preparation. It was these combined circumstances, together with the difficulties that breeders had to contend with in order to produce a spotless white animal, that were largely responsible for the dog's downfall. Then, too, it must not be forgotten that the rise into favour of varieties whose coats

Type of English White Terrier.

required less labour to keep them in nice condition also contributed to the decadence. Long after England had practically ceased to produce any specimens worthy of the old traditions, Scotland possessed one or two fanciers who stuck manfully to the breed and only forsook it when they found that it was hopelessly in the van.

Constituent Parts.

When first known to the writer it was altogether a heavier-made dog than is the English White Terrier of to-day, and there were then more external evidences of one constituent that had been used in its " manufacture "—the Bull-Terrier. Still, though there are many surmises as to the crosses that had been resorted to in order to produce this Terrier, it is mere conjecture at this date to state that it contained the blood of Whippet, Fox-Terrier, and Bull-Terrier. Lancashire and Warwick were the counties in which the best specimens of the old dogs were met with, and it was not at all uncommon to see the reflex of the Whippet cross—wheel back and hooped tail; while the mincing gait that was sometimes a feature seemed to suggest even a dash of Italian Greyhound. The modern breeder has got rid of these objectionable characteristics to a very large extent, and the dog breeds fairly true to type. Another defect oftener met with in the older specimens than in those of more recent times is deafness, though this is, as in all white animals—white cats are often deaf—very liable to occur.

Constitution and Temperament.

By nature the English White Terrier must be regarded as delicate, and on account of the scanty coat it is necessary to keep it clothed when exposed to anything like cold weather. Added to which it has been very closely in-bred to preserve fixity of type; and this is another factor responsible for lack of robustness, and an outcross is certainly suggested. As regards temperament the breed leaves nothing to be desired; and the same may be said in respect of its qualities as a house-dog and companion. Still, as is the case with white dogs generally, there is an objection, more especially in big towns and cities, as the coats soon show signs of dirt, necessitating a good deal of labour to keep them in the pink of condition. Against that, however, so far as this Terrier is concerned, may be set its undoubted smartness, activity, and generally symmetrical appearance.

Preparation for Show.

As in the case of the larger Bull-Terrier, a good deal of preparation is required over and above that which such a short-coated variety would seem to suggest. The very fine tail and clean-cut face are often not products of Nature, but are the result of artificial cultivation at the hands of the expert, who continues to practise the art despite the fact that such acts have been pronounced illegal. Washing just prior to a show, followed by a good hand-rubbing to minimise the ill-effects that the order of the bath constantly conferred is calculated to produce, thorough brushing at all times, and

Spratt's Patent Brush and Powder Distributor for Dry-cleaning
White Dogs.

sufficient exercise to maintain its symmetry, constitute the chief preparation of this dog for show.

As with the Bull-Terrier so with its near relative the English White Terrier there seems to be a predisposition for the skin to redden in certain parts, particularly if unduly exposed. This may lead to skin trouble if not guarded against by the use of a coat, as previously mentioned. Some fanciers instead of washing use a dry-cleaning powder and brush. Spratt's Patent sell a combination brush and powder distributor for such a purpose. If this be resorted to in the case of a show-dog, the greatest care must be taken to remove every particle of the cleaning agent, or disqualifi-. cation will result for a certainty. Still, if the soap be chosen with care, no dry-cleaning agent yet known is as efficient as washing. All that one needs to remember in the latter connection is that in the final rinsing water a little of the housekeeper's blue-bag should be used. This imparts that whiteness so desirable.

Selecting a Puppy,

So many nowadays prefer to start with a puppy, that it may be as well to state that an apple-headed specimen, or one showing Bull-Terrier conformation should be rejected, as should also a patched or even a slightly-marked specimen. Light eyes, an under-shot or an over-shot mouth, long back, and a long tail are other defects.

Description.

The following is a description of the variety, as drawn up by the English White Terrier Club, of which Mr. J. H. Walsh, one of the most successful of modern fanciers, was for some time honorary secretary :—

Head.—Long and narrow, flat from the back of the skull to the nose, and with no bumps at sides or cheeks.

Muzzle.—Long and tapering, but not weak.

Jaws.—Strong, teeth close-fitting and even, with no lippiness.

Eyes.—Small, oval shaped, bright in expression, and dark, nearly black, in colour.

Nose.—Well defined, quite black, and of moderate size.

Ears.—Small, fine in texture, V-shaped, and hanging close to the head.

Neck.—Light and graceful, rather long, slightly arched.

Shoulders.—Sloping ; chest rather narrow, but deep.

Body.—A little arched, with good back ribs.

Fore Legs.—Quite straight, with well-arched toes and black nails.

Hindquarters.—Strong and powerful, with hocks well let down.

Tail.—Very fine, and carried almost straight or with a slight curve, but never curled over the back.

Coat.—Short, fine, and glossy.

Colour.—Pure white.

Weight.—Should not exceed 20lb., even less is desirable.

General Appearance.—That of a well-bred and high-class, smart and neat-looking dog, well suited for a companion or a house-guard.

STANDARD OF EXCELLENCE.

Head, including Jaws	20
Ears	10
Eyes	5
Legs and Feet	10
Body and Quarters	10
Colour	20
Tail	5
General appearance (including size) and action	20
Total	100

THE FOX-TERRIER.

The Breed as a Whole.

ALIKE on the score of numbers, popularity, and monetary value, the Fox-Terrier, as a breed, may be legitimately considered an easy first when compared with any other Terrier; while it is also rightly regarded as the most popular of all Domestic Dogs, the only breeds running it at all close being the Collie and the Bulldog. For over a quarter of a century the breed has held almost undisputed sway, and even in the twentieth century there are not many signs of a waning popularity. The breed is divided by fanciers into two varieties, differentiated only by the coat, the one being designated Smooth-Haired and the other Wire-Haired. The former is without doubt the more popular variety, though the latter of recent years has come on apace. As dogs for general purposes there is absolutely nothing to choose between the two varieties, though there are, of course, individuals in both that on their merits would seem to give to one or the other a superiority.

The Smooth-Haired.

Origin.

Though it is useful, if not, indeed, absolutely necessary, to give some slight idea as to the origin of at any rate those breeds which may be said to go back a century or two, yet no good purpose would be served by endeavouring to trace the gradual evolution of this breed. Those requiring such historical data will find them in the monographs published respectively by Mr. Horace Cox and Mr. L. Upcott Gill. For the present purpose it will be sufficient to say that the present-day Fox-Terrier sprang from the strains of Kennel Terriers associated with such packs as the Grove, Belvoir, Lord Middleton's, and a few others; while there were also individuals like Mr. Gibson, Mr. Burbidge, Mr. Doyle, Mr. A. H. Clarke, Mr. J. C. Tinne, Mr. Vicary, Mr. Francis Redmond, and a host of others who continued the good work of moulding the

Type of Smooth Fox-Terrier—Mr Houlker's Adam Bede.

materials they had to hand, until the dog as we know it to-day was gradually evolved. Generally it is thought that the Fox-Terrier in the early days was a black-and-tan dog, but built on very different lines from the Terrier that we know by such a name. Be that as it may, we find little trace of it beyond markings in the Fox-Terrier of 1862—a date that marks an epoch in the breed, for it was in that year that Birmingham first provided for the variety a separate classification, and that may be said to be the starting-point of the dog's popularity. Since that time it has scarcely

ever looked back, while *the* club which fosters its interests
is one of the oldest of all canine institutions, being, as regards
years, second only to the Kennel Club itself.

Ups and Downs.

Of necessity, a breed which for show purposes alone
has existed for half-a-century or more must have had its
ups and downs, even if there were no periods when its
position as regards the dog-loving public gave its admirers
cause for anxiety. In the transitional stages from a purely
Kennel Terrier to that of a fashionable beauty, a good
many rough corners had to be knocked off the breed, and
a good deal of type adjustment had to be made in order
to convert the one into the other. Better housing, feeding,
exercising, and grooming also were not without their
influences, and gradually a smarter dog with smaller ears,
shorter back, longer legs, more compact feet, and better
points was evolved. In doing so the size was increased
considerably, and for a long time it looked as if the
breed would, on account of its bulk, be quite useless for
the purpose for which it was originally intended, namely,
to go to earth to fox. This went on for some time,
until Mr. Shirley at one of the Fox-Terrier Club's gatherings
suddenly upset all calculations by going for the good " little
'uns," and from that time there has been no serious attempt
to introduce the big dogs that were at one time the fashion.
Still, the big dog must not be lightly regarded if over-size
be its only fault. It may be, and indeed is, possible so to
utilise the dog or the bitch that it may be of the greatest
value to the breeder—that is, when he or she understands the
fundamental laws that govern this function.

Breeding Hints.

As the Fox-Terrier is the most popular of all Terriers,
it is proposed to deal with a few points here that, while they
will be particularly appropriate to the variety under discus-

sion, will apply with equal force to all other varieties. First as to the selection of the bitch : there is a common fallacy existing among novices in dog-breeding that any moderate bitch is good enough to breed from, so long as she is healthy and mated to a sire excelling where she is deficient. All that need be said here is that in actual practice it will not work. The bitch, contrary to the general belief, exerts just as much influence on the future progeny as the sire ; probably more. Simply to choose a bitch for breeding whose only qualifications are that she comes of a good strain would be the way *not* to breed successfully. It is here that the majority of novices stumble. Rather should their aim be to pay extra attention to the bitch, seeing that she is called upon not only to combine with the sire in producing certain externals, but also to nourish the puppies as well. A much-exhibited bitch would not be the best of mothers as a rule, inasmuch as she would necessarily lead a more or less strenuous life in being prepared for the shows and travelling many hundreds or perhaps thousands of miles under conditions not conducive to health.

Other points that should engage the attention of the prospective breeder are :—(1) That of allowing half-grown bitches to be mated. It is absolutely impossible for a dam to build up her own frame and to nourish the whelps in the fœtus without causing a most serious strain upon her own economy, and also without weakening constitutionally the progeny yet unborn. (2) Whether it is better to start with a maiden bitch or one that has already exercised her maternal functions. The weight of common sense is on the side of the latter choice—namely, of a known quantity, her power to reproduce her kind, rather than an altogether unknown one. It is necessary also to go a step further and to find out, when laying the foundation of a kennel, whether the stock from which the dam springs is one that gives promise of success with the matrons composing it. Then, again, a brood bitch should not be allowed to breed twice in a season ; nor is it advisable for a beginner to keep a stud dog. This last is suggested by the number of times that the question has been put to the writer. It cannot be too often explained that all the best stud dogs in the country are at the service of the public, and the chance of a sire, however good, being suited to every individual bitch that is to be found in even a small kennel is so remote as scarcely to be worth considering.

To found a successful kennel of Terriers of any kind is a most difficult task, and not to be accomplished quickly unless the prospective owner is prepared to expend some very large sums on this phase of his hobby. In the past, vast sums have been given for brood bitches and stud dogs by Lord Lonsdale, who fancied the Wire-Hairs, and by Mr. S. J. Stephens, who favoured the Smooths ; and though, in the one case, at any rate, partial success was achieved, there was apparently not sufficient to justify the extension of the experiment. Whether a man is about to lay the foundation of a Smooth- or a Wire-Haired kennel, he must at the outset make up his mind to encounter some disappointments. The best plan is first of all to gain some practical experience of the breed, a knowledge of strains, and then to look around for a brood bitch or two wherewith to commence. There have been dozens of successful fanciers whose total outlay probably did not exceed the modest £10, but whose practical judgment and discernment enabled them to buy the best article in the best market. Even the foundation of such a world-famous strain of Fox-Terrier as the Russell was started by a purchase from a country milkman! Contrast this with the phenomenally large sums referred to elsewhere. The fame of the one, too, was as short-lived as that of the other was enduring.

It matters not whether a Fox-Terrier is to be purchased for its working or its show-ring qualities, "blood will tell." The prospective kennel-owner must therefore keep this point well in mind. A bitch that is a descendant of a strain of workers or of show-dogs is far more likely to transmit the qualities desired than one which is simply good-looking

or that shows excellent working characteristics by accident,
as it were. Now and again opportunities for securing first-class stock at public auction occur; but they are at
such rare intervals as scarcely to be worth consideration.
Selling-classes at shows may also be dismissed as being unlikely to yield promising material to the purchaser. As a
matter of fact, the best mediums are the columns of the newspapers giving place to kennel advertisements; or, failing to
obtain what is required by such means, then there are plenty
of breeders of repute who may be relied upon to furnish first-
class stock at fair prices. It is the person who in these days
expects to get something for nothing that is destined (and
deserves) to be disappointed. Far too many young fanciers
seem to be under the erroneous impression that any pedigree
dog must necessarily be a good one. The sooner this is
dissipated the better. That pedigree is an important factor
for consideration in a purchase is of course admitted; but it
is a factor to be taken into consideration with the individual
offered. Again, there are pedigrees *and* pedigrees. A
mere string of dogs' names without any connecting links is
of absolutely no value. It is also very necessary in this
connection to make sure of all the facts in any pedigree before concluding a purchase and not after; and this, of
course, applies to every breed of dog.

A Profitable Breed.

A very large proportion of those who keep the highest
class of Fox-Terrier do so without any regard as to whether
or not the hobby is a remunerative one. They like the companionship and sport it affords, whether this latter be in the
pursuit of its legitimate calling or in the more restricted show-
ring. Still, there are many others who have first to consider
before seriously taking up a breed whether it is likely to
pay its way or even to yield a profit.

That being so, the question Is the Fox-Terrier a profitable breed to keep? may be one that we may reasonably

anticipate, more especially as it is the most popular of all
Terriers, as already suggested, if, indeed, it be not of all
dogs.   To such a question we are disposed to reply in the
affirmative so long as the breeding and rearing are conducted
on business and practical lines, and not too much money is
expended at the outset.   Before, however, anyone can reasonably hope to make the hobby pay he must have gained a
reputation for breeding good dogs as opposed to buying
them.   Moreover, he must have proved beyond a reasonable
doubt that he is capable of producing dogs of sufficient calibre
to hold their own in open competition.   Having thus established his claim to be considered a practical dog-breeder, he
should soon see some good results so far as his exchequer is
concerned.   The profit that is likely to accrue from a good
kennel of Fox-Terriers is not so much to be derived from the
young progeny that he rears as from the substantial stud-fees
that are likely to come in should he be sufficiently fortunate
to possess a dog or two whose show record justly entitles
them to be in demand by breeders.   If, moreover, with their
show record they have an additional one for siring good
puppies, success so far as the owner is concerned should be
assured.   To own a few good Fox-Terriers got together by
the outlay of a certain number of pounds is one thing.   To
breed them and to keep them on such lines that they can
hold their own in open competition quite another.

As showing what it is possible for an experienced Fox-
Terrier breeder to make even by winnings at a single show,
we may quote a rather remarkable performance in this direction achieved by Mr. Francis Redmond at one of the Fox-
Terrier Club's shows in 1897.   That gentleman won at a single
meeting nearly £250 in hard cash, together with two special
cups and the fifty-guinea challenge cup!   This, of course,
was a phenomenal win, and Mr. Francis Redmond is universally acknowledged as one of the foremost breeders of
the popular Terrier.   Still, it goes to prove that even if
experience has to be bought by the novice, as it admittedly
does, it pays in the end.

"Weeding Out."

This process is a very necessary one wherever puppies are bred. Those who go in for rearing show stock do not, of course, hastily discard any but obvious deformities or absolutely mismarked specimens. On the other hand, those whose aim is to breed just companionable animals weed out the youngsters at the earliest possible moment that they can do with safety, and prefer to sell them while they are in the " pretty " stage—from seven weeks or so old. Not so, as we have already stated, the Fox-Terrier breeder for show. He prefers to place the puppies out " at walk " until such times as the weeding-out process may be undertaken without any mistake being made. Light-eyed, flesh-colour nosed specimens would be got rid of at once, as these would not be desirable for either show or stock, generally speaking, unless the defect were just an accident of birth and did not throw back to any family influence. It is not at all uncommon with Terriers in general for the ears of puppies at a certain stage to seem out of keeping with the rest of the body. This should not be taken too seriously, as we have had Terriers exhibit this and yet when they were properly " furnished " the ears were in the correct proportion to the head. Puppies with under-shot or over-shot mouths should also be discarded, as either of these is, we think, a fatal *defect in any Terrier*. Markings in the Fox Terrier are of no particular import, and we have, moreover, elsewhere referred to them. Should any leg-deformities be noticed, such as are not uncommon with rickets, these will not be likely to be remedied: hence the puppies would be useless for show.

Tail-Docking and Dew-Claws.

The Fox-Terrier is one of the Terriers that Fashion has decreed shall be docked of a portion of their tails, and it is almost unnecessary to state that unless a dog that is required for show is so treated it stands absolutely no chance of " catching the judge's eye." Though but a minor operation, as now

E

performed, yet at one time it was the very common practice to
bite off the tail, this being considered the only way in which a
really good " dock " could be obtained. In those days tails
were docked much shorter than now. The disgusting practice of biting, though it has practically disappeared, still
finds adherents in very remote parts of the country. The
operation is best performed while the puppies are under a
week old, removing not quite half the tail. There are in vogue
various methods of doing this, some calculated to induce a
better tail-carriage than others. The skin and hair should
first be gently pushed back, and then, with a fairly sharp
knife, the portion to be removed cut all round, but not
quite through, and the tendon drawn out. Some fanciers
prefer a pair of nippers for this purpose. Generally
speaking, no styptic of any kind is required, the dam's
tongue doing all that is needful. Docking, it may be as
well to state, is an illegal operation.

" Dew-claws," as they are termed, occur in every breed,
and should always be cut off. Not only when removed is a
cleaner appearance imparted to the leg, but the dog is saved
not a little pain, as in his gambols when older he is sure
to get them torn. The best time for their removal is during
the first few days of puppyhood. A pair of surgical scissors
should be used, and the claw and skin so held that just a
snip in an upward direction suffices to remove them, leaving
but a very small wound. This may be touched with tincture
of matico, Friar's balsam, and Battley's solution of opium
in equal parts.

" Walking " Puppies.

It is almost the universal practice of Fox-Terrier
breeders of note not to attempt to rear the puppies at home.
The risk is far too great, apart from the undoubted
fact that puppies, when put out to walk in pairs,
thrive twice as well as when five or six are allowed to be
reared to an age when their future may with certainty be

determined. This necessarily adds to the cost, but it is money well expended.

The exhibition of young puppies on the off-chance of securing a prize is a practice that cannot be too strongly condemned, and many a promising youngster has had its career prematurely cut short through indulging in what is always a risky proceeding.

Preparation for Show.

Although the Smooth Fox-Terrier requires little preparation for show as compared with its Wire-Haired relative, yet it must not be thought that anything will do. It is a moot point amongst breeders whether a bath, dry-cleaning, or a spirit-wash is the best method of coat-cleaning. So far as the first-named is concerned, there can scarcely be two opinions that washing has a more or less deleterious effect upon the coat, unless the soap be free from strong alkalies and a good deal of vigorous hand-rubbing is indulged in after the bath. Where Fox-Terriers are living in towns, the coat and skin are bound to get more or less grimy, and no dry-cleaning agent yet devised can so well remove the dirt and allow the skin to perform its proper functions as washing. Baked flour, bran, and the other much-vaunted agents may be used to remove a soiled spot in a coat ; but they cannot exert a cleansing effect on the skin. Of late years there has been devised what may be termed a spirit wash or a shampoo wash (Sherley's, for instance) that may be more safely employed than soap and water-blue. It combines, also, cleansing with insecticidal properties. Moreover, in the case of soap and water a good deal of grooming after the tub is necessary, for if the dog be returned to its bed in a half-dried state, there is a tendency for the coat to be wavier than is desirable. This is largely obviated with the spirit-washes referred to.

So far as actual grooming is concerned, this is best performed with the slanting-bristle brush already referred to and illustrated (see under " Airedale Terrier "). This should

E 2

be performed each day. Many Smooth Fox-Terriers suffer from a scanty coat—some are so thin as more to resemble that of a Bull-Terrier. This may be remedied to a certain extent by keeping the dog under less artificial conditions than sometimes prevail. A dog, for instance, that was allowed to pass a good deal of its time in the house would be better if kept under cooler conditions outside, even if for a time it be necessary for the animal to wear a coat. Still, no amount of treatment will convert a soft-textured coat into one of the requisite degree of hardness. There are certain hardening mediums—alum, for instance—employed by the fraudulent to impart a temporary hardness. Still nothing but improved natural conditions will permanently harden the coat, and no one of repute would descend to such a deceit, and even if he did, the chances are that he would soon be discovered.

Exercise in the case of the Fox-Terrier does not differ from that necessary for any other similar Terrier : road walking is best, as it imparts to legs, feet, and muscles an appearance of fitness not to be obtained by any other means. To give fast exercise behind cycle, cart, or other vehicle is calculated to spoil the shape of the feet.

Though the washing of a Terrier is a comparatively simple operation, yet there are some who do not know how to proceed, or that there is a right and a wrong way of performing it. Lukewarm water to which just a little household ammonia (two table-spoonfuls to five or six gallons of water) has been added, and a first-class soap, such as that sold by Garstin, will soon cleanse the dog. The body and legs should be done first, and the head last. Similarly, if one of the shampoo washes be employed, the method will in no wise differ. After all the dirt has been removed the dog must be rinsed, and in the final rinsing-water the blue-bag should be squeezed. This imparts a far more desirable whiteness than is obtainable from soap and water only. Having allowed the dog to get rid of some of the water, the drying must be proceeded with.

The Kennel Club Rules are very specific as to what may and what may not be legitimately done in the way of "preparation." Before, therefore, making the attempt it would be advisable to read these through carefully.

Ear-Carriage.

With Terriers generally there is often a good deal of trouble experienced as regards the carriage of the ears, and the Fox-Terriers are no exception to the rule. In the past there is no room to doubt that many malpractices were resorted to in order to give an imperfectly-carried ear the correct carriage on the eventful day. So far as show-dogs are concerned, these are now things of the past, although owners have none the less an anxious time with their dogs now and again in consequence of a refractory ear. The general tendency is for an ear to "prick" instead of to lie close to the head, and when this is the case it is well gently to manipulate the ear between finger and thumb several times a day. By so doing the ear may after a time be correctly carried unless the defect is a permanent one, when nothing legitimately may be done. By the Rules of the Kennel Club weighting, once considered permissible, is not allowed, although it is difficult to see how this can be prevented if the traces of the "lozenge," or whatever is used, are carefully removed before the dog is required to be shown.

Amateurs breeding puppies for the first time often betray too much concern for an indifferently-carried ear. It is a well-known fact that very young puppies of all breeds not infrequently carry both ears and tails indifferently until the teething process is complete. For this reason, if for no other, it would be quite unsafe to discard such puppies until, say, they were over six months old. If when well over this age it is found that the correct ear-carriage is not assumed it may safely be concluded that the case is practically hopeless.

As there will be many complete novices amongst those reading this work, it may be well to put them on their guard against some of the shady practices that are occasionally indulged in by those not having any particular reputation at stake. We say occasionally, as cases are far fewer than they were even ten years ago. When buying in the " open market " novices should carefully examine the ears of any prospective purchases, and if there are any scars or suspicious marks upon them such dogs should be left severely alone. Of course, it is quite possible to come by such marks in the course of a fight; but when this is offered as an explanation it must be taken in conjunction with other circumstances. Dropping-ears was at one time a common and doubtless a fairly profitable practice. Again, even should there be no actual marks on the ears, these organs should be felt with finger and thumb, and if whipcord-like ridges are found these, too, should be regarded at least with suspicion.

Markings.

One of the points in which amateur fanciers frequently need enlightenment is that of marking. The description of the breed specifically states : " White should predominate ; brindle, red, or liver markings are objectionable ; otherwise the point is of little importance." Not so long ago markings (even if they were of the orthodox colours) were considered objectionable if at all heavy. The unfairness, however, of handicapping an otherwise good dog, for what, after all, is of minor import, must have occurred to those who in Fox-Terrier circles were regarded as the " censors," and one well remembers the comments that were rife when certain heavily-marked dogs were winning freely. Personally, other things being equal, we are of opinion that the black-and-tan head is far and away the most attractive marking that any Smooth Fox-Terrier can possess, the rest of the body being white. For all that, a breeder must not hastily dispose of an otherwise promising puppy from a litter purely on the score that the markings are those that

are tabooed in the description issued by the Fox-Terrier Club.
The markings may be one of those accidental individual
variations from the type that are liable to occur in every
breed. If on looking into the family-tree of the individual
so marked it were found that the blemish (if so it may be
called) was not one found on the family escutcheon, then in
the case of a bitch there is no reason why she should not
be used for breeding from.

Uses, &c.

Primarily the Fox-Terrier, as its name and origin
sufficiently indicate, was a working dog kept for the purpose
of " bolting " the fox from his earth, not, as is commonly
thought, of killing him. To-day, so far as the majority
of show specimens are concerned, they are fashionable
beauties, far too valuable to run any such risk. But it
must not be deduced therefrom that they have lost that
gameness that was a characteristic of the early progenitor—
the Kennel Terrier. To-day there are to be found Fox-
Terriers every bit as game and as good at vermin as any
that did duty with the Belvoir or other crack pack. Moreover, it is fairly well known that several of our foremost
Fox-Terrier breeders are in the habit of placing their puppies
" at walk " with gamekeepers, by whom they are entered
to vermin of sorts.

Apart from the show section of the dog-loving community, there is a very large public that keep the Fox-
Terrier for the combined purpose of companionship, sport,
and household guards, and right excellently they perform
their part. For alertness, Fox-Terriers generally have no
superiors amongst the Terriers ; while with very little training
they may be made to restrain the hard-biting nature that
characterises them and to become very useful aids to the
sportsman. White, too, largely preponderating, they are
far more useful in questing than many other Terriers
that at a distance are not readily seen, and which, there-

fore, stand a good chance of being shot. As a water-dog
it may be classed as excellent; while added to all it boasts
a sound constitution and a capital temperament, albeit in
the show-ring it is a trifle " snarly." It is not proposed here
to enter into the many phases of sport in which the Fox-
Terrier may be used or the training necessary to him therefor.
This will be dealt with in the next volume in a section
specially devoted to the subject.

Toy Fox-Terriers.

To dwarf certain breeds seems to be the chief aim of
many interested in dogs, and the latest breed to have a pocket
edition of the larger article is the popular Fox-Terrier. To
produce a miniature in any of the breeds is not particularly
difficult, but to produce one that is typical and capable of
reproducing its kind is quite another matter.

Clubs.

To but few breeds is it given to have so many clubs
to look after their interests as the Fox-Terrier has, for
besides the parent society there are no fewer than ten others.
Added to which the breed boasts a literature of its own in
the various monographs and an excellent series of Stud Books
commenced by the late Mr. Hugh Dalziel and continued by
the Fox-Terrier Club.

Description of Breed.

The following is the description of the Smooth Fox-
Terrier as drawn up by the Fox-Terrier Club just named :—

Head.—The skull should be flat and moderately narrow; broader
between the ears, and gradually decreasing in width to the eyes.
Not much "stop" should be apparent; but there should be more
dip in the profile, between the forehead and top jaw, than is seen in
the case of a Greyhound. The ears should be V-shaped, and rather
small; of moderate thickness, and dropping forward closely to the
cheek, not hanging by the side of the head, like a Foxhound's. The
jaw should be strong and muscular, but not too full in the cheek; it

should be of fair punishing length, but not so as in any way to resemble the Greyhound's or modern English Terrier's. There should not be much falling away below the eyes; this part of the head should, however, be moderately chiselled out, so as not to go down in a straight slope like a wedge. The nose, towards which the muzzle must slightly taper, should be black. The eyes should be dark-rimmed, small, and rather deep set; full of fire and life. The teeth should be level and strong.

Neck should be clean and muscular, without throatiness, of fair length, and gradually widening to the shoulders.

Shoulders should be fine at the points, long, and sloping. The chest deep, and not broad.

Back should be short, straight, and strong, with no appearance of slackness behind the shoulders; the loin broad, powerful, and very slightly arched. The dog should be well ribbed up with deep back ribs and should not be flat-sided.

Hindquarters should be strong and muscular, quite free from droop or crouch; the thighs long and powerful; hocks near the ground, the dog standing well up on them like a Foxhound, without much bend in the stifles.

Stern should be set on rather high, and carried gaily; but not over the back, or curled. It should be of good strength, anything approaching a pipe-stopper tail being especially objectionable.

Legs, viewed in any direction, must be straight, showing little or no appearance of ankle in front. They should be large in bone throughout, the elbows working freely just clear of the side. Both fore and hind legs should be carried straight forward in travelling, the stifles not turning outwards. The feet should be round, compact, and not too large; the toes moderately arched, and turned neither in nor out. There should be no dew-claws behind.

The *Coat* should be smooth, but hard, dense, and abundant.

Colour.—White should predominate. Brindle, red, or liver markings are objectionable. Otherwise this point is of little or no importance.

Symmetry, Size, and Character.—The dog must present a generally gay, lively, and active appearance. Bone and strength in a small compass are essentials; but this must not be taken to mean that a Fox-Terrier should be "cloggy," or in any way coarse. Speed and endurance must be looked to as well as power, and the symmetry of the Foxhound taken as a model. The Terrier, like the Hound, must on no account be leggy; neither must he be too short in the leg. He should stand like a cleverly made hunter—covering a lot of ground, yet with a short back, as before stated. He will thus attain the highest degree of propelling power, together with the greatest length of stride that is compatible with the length of his body. Weight is not a certain criterion of a Terrier's fitness for his work. General shape, size, and contour are the main points; and if a dog can gallop and stay, and follow his fox, it matters little what his weight is to a pound or so, though, roughly speaking, it may be said that he should not scale over 20lb. in show condition.

The Wire-Haired.

Early Days.

Although the Wire-Haired Fox-Terrier has probably existed as long as its Smooth relative, growing up side by side with it as it were, yet for a long time it made little or no progress. Indeed, it was regarded somewhat unfavourably even by those who were lovers of dogs, and it was not at all uncommon to associate the Wire-Haired Fox-Terrier of the early days as a fitting companion only for the itinerant tinker or the village rat-catcher. Little wonder, therefore, that the Smooth romped away from its Broken-haired relative, and was flourishing exceedingly long ere the latter had even obtained the hall-mark of a variety by being included in the Kennel Club Stud-Book classification. For all that, at the beginning of the nineteenth century, if no earlier, there were strains—and known strains, too—of this useful variety kept pure, and valued almost exclusively for their working capabilities. Of such was the Russell strain (of the 'sixties in the last century), associated with the hunting parson of that name; and there were others which, if they never attained the same celebrity, were at any rate scarcely less worthy as workers.

As showing how little the Wire-Haired Fox-Terrier was thought of, it may be stated that prior to 1872 it was the custom to exhibit them with a more or less miscellaneous lot

of " Broken-Haired Terriers " ; and even after some of the
executives of the more important fixtures deemed it advisable
to provide a separate classification, it was not until some
years later that the breed had the *locus standi* so far as
the Kennel Club was concerned. Moreover, at one time it
was classed as a non-sporting dog! Now if ever there was
a breed of Terrier that deserved to be classed as a sporting

Type of Wire-Haired Fox-Terrier—Mr. J. D. Dudson's Champion
Briar Sportsman.

one it was the Wire-Haired Fox-Terrier ; while the only
acknowledged difference then or now between the two
varieties was and is one of coat. To the Northern
breeders chiefly we are indebted for the blood
of our best Wire-Haired Fox-Terriers, the districts
around Cleveland, Carlisle, and Darlington being especially
noteworthy ; while of the earlier breeders that we at the

same time associate with shows none were better known than
Mr. W. Carrick, whose Tack (an illustration of which is
given for purposes of comparison with present-day types)
and Tyro are pillars of the Stud Book; Mr. T. Wooton
(the owner in his time of some of the best), Mr. A. H.
Easten, Mr. G. F. Richardson, Mr. S. E. Shirley, and
a dozen or so more, including such well-known enthusiasts
as Mr. Hayward Field, Mr. Maxwell, Mr. Harding Cox,
Messrs. Maxwell and Cassel, Mr. Lindsay Hogg, &c.
Despite, however, an excellent following, the breed did
not make much headway; nor was there the same uniformity of type shown as in the Smooths.   About 1894
the breed took its rightful place, and to-day, as regards
popularity, there is little to choose between the Smooth-
and the Wire-Haired Fox-Terrier.   Moreover, the latter
holds the record as regards price, no less a sum than £500
each having been paid for two specimens—Champion
Meersbrook Bristles and Champion Gobang!

Hindrances to Further Progress.

With all the progress made by the breed there have
nevertheless been at work causes which militated considerably
against its further popularity.   It is no secret that, compared
with its Smooth-Haired relative, the Wire-Haired Dog
requires a great deal more show preparation.   In fact, to
get ready one of these Terriers, if it is successfully to
compete against the " talent," the services of a professional
trainer must be enlisted.   Now, it is the glorious uncertainty
as to how far a breeder may go in the direction of tittivating
a coat without actually falling under the designation of a
faker that has prevented numbers, as in the case of the
Bedlington Terrier, from taking up the breed.   The Kennel
Club distinctly says that the " fast coat " must not be
removed; but he would be a clever man indeed who could
prepare many of the Wire-Hairs according to the tenets
of the fancy without so doing.   Therefore, while on the

one hand trimming is discouraged, on the other it is
tacitly admitted. Breeders, of course, are steadily improving
coats, and in the near future there should be little need for
wholesale trimming.

Crossing the Two Varieties.

Another of the vexed questions in connection with this
breed is whether it is in the best interests of the two varieties

Old Type of Wire-Haired Fox-Terrier—Mr. Carrick's Carlisle Tack (late Tack).

to inter-cross them, as by some has been done in the past.
The immediate effect of such a cross upon the progeny of
any individual may be, perhaps, to remove what in the eyes
of the fancy may be considered a blemish—a slight curl
in the coat; but breeders have really to consider what its
effect will be hereafter. To judge by results achieved so

far, it looks as if the crossing of Wire-Haired with Smooth-
Haired was, in many instances, of decided utility.   Still,
is not there the danger of reversion to be feared?   We should
think so if one is to judge by certain fundamental laws
that govern breeding.   For years the two varieties have
been kept apart, each breeding more or less true to type.
All of a sudden some astute fancier, in deference to a change
in fashion, probably as radical as it was undesirable,
conceives the idea of improving coats by a quick-change
process.   We must personally confess to having experimented in the direction suggested, but, at the same time, to
having doubts as to the effect in the future.   All that we
can point to are the present-day successes : the future has
yet to be revealed.

Show Preparation.

The author who imagines that by any word-description he
can more than point the way to the preparation of this very
business-like-looking Terrier is, to say the least, labouring
under a great delusion.   At different times specimens of
the breed have passed through the writer's hands, for which
sums varying from £5 to £50 have been paid, and the
jackets have varied in a like ratio.   The fact is, one
specimen will need a lot of trimming (on the little-and-often
principle) to produce the show-ring coat, while another may
be prepared with very little trouble.   As we have frequently
stated, each individual is, in respect of show preparation,
a law unto itself.   Of one thing the novice may be quite
certain—namely, that, though it may be voted " faking "
to remove the coat of the show dog in various unorthodox
ways, unless he does so, or, what is better, employs someone
else to, he might as well keep that Terrier at home for any
chance he may stand of " catching the judge's eye."   If
any prospective exhibitor, buying the very best stock that
money will secure, relies upon grooming, as ordinarily
understood, to stand his dog in good stead on the eventful

day, he is destined to have his senses rudely awakened.
Many of our Wire-Haired Terriers, if allowed to sport their
natural coats, would present a very different appearance from
the smartened dog of the show-ring. A professional
trimmer taking on hand such a dog about a month or so
before it was required to be shown could so alter its
appearance for the better that scarcely anyone seeing it
before " the treatment " would recognise it after as the same
dog. The business is a ticklish one, and especially careful
has the trimmer to be of the hair immediately in front of
the eyes and in the vicinity of the muzzle. By removing,
say, a little too much of the hair near the latter he may
impart a look of snipiness that would not have been so
palpable had the moustache-like hair been judiciously
employed for covering up the defect. Similarly, too, an
additional length of head may be imparted by careful
trimming right down the cheeks, though not by means of
clippers, as is sometimes done. Once the general public are
made aware of the practices resorted to and tacitly allowed,
it rests with them to compete or not with the " old hands."
Still, either " trimming," as now conducted, should be
admittedly allowed in all breeds or it should be treated as
" faking " and dealt with accordingly. So far as the other
preparation is concerned, what has been said in that connection under the Smooth-Haired variety will apply equally to
this. A novice, in purchasing in the open market, must take
care that he does not pick up one of the much-trimmed
specimens got up with a view to deceive. He should especially regard with suspicion a smart-looking one that has soft
hair on the poll or on the legs or feet. Not a few
Wire-Hairs having Smooth blood in them show this undesirable softness of coat.

Russell Strain.

No section on the Wire-Haired Fox Terrier could be
considered complete that did not refer in something more

than a casual way to the famous strain that is indelibly
associated with the name of the Rev. Jack Russell. To the
present generation of Fox-Terrier men—or, at any rate, the
majority—the type of dog is but a name. Still, there can
be no room for doubt as to its working qualities : these are
writ large in the annals of Devonshire foxhunting. Moreover, in the very excellent memorial work " Dartmoor Days,"
the very history of the founding of the strain is given. The
pity is that so fine a strain of dog was allowed to die out, or
practically so, for there are few breeders, even in the West,
who can boast the blood in their dogs. The late Mr. Henry
East, of Chislehurst, himself a M.F.H., kept some dogs in
which the blood of the Russell strain coursed ; and, so far as
we can recollect, he was the only breeder near London to
possess it.

The strain was founded in quite a casual way, and during
the undergraduate days of Mr. Russell at Oxford. The
bitch from which the stock was produced was purchased of
a Marston milkman, with whom the young Oxford student
chanced to meet while on a walk. Of the progeny that in
after years became so famous in the hunting-field we can
have no better description than that furnished by the writer
of the " Memoir " already noted. He says that they were
" as steady from riot as the staunchest of his [Russell's]
hounds, so that running together with them, and never passing over an earth without drawing it, they gave a fox,
whether above ground or below it, but a poor chance of not
being found by one or the other."

Russell, though occasionally judging at shows, including
the Kennel Club's own fixture, was apparently not greatly
in love with the Fox-Terrier as ordinarily bred for the purpose, and, so far as we can gather, his dogs were seldom, if
at all, exhibited. For all that it must not be supposed that
they were not as good to look at as they were game in the
field, and, if we are to judge by the admirable picture of
them that the author of " Dartmoor Days " affords, they
would have won had they been exhibited in the present day,

especially now that the craze for the big Fox-Terrier has practically subsided. Trump, the bitch that was destined to lay the foundation of a famous strain, is thus described. She was " white, with just a patch of dark tan over each ear ; while a similar dot, not larger than a penny piece, marked the root of the tail. The coat was thick and close, and a trifle wiry, and calculated to protect the body from cold, but had no affinity with the long, rough jacket of a Scotch Terrier. The forelegs were as straight as arrows, the feet perfect, the loins and conformation of the whole frame indicative of hardihood and endurance ; while the size and height were comparable to those of a full-grown vixen fox."

As so many seem to be under the impression that the Rev. Jack Russell had little to do with the world of dogs outside his own particular county, it may be interesting to quote some particulars concerning him from Mr. Jaquet's monumental " History of the Kennel Club." After referring to some of the earlier members of the Kennel Club, whose names were " household words " in connection with dog-breeding, he says : " One of the first of these was the Rev. John Russell, of Barnstaple, the Sporting Parson, better known as ' Jack ' Russell. He joined the Club in 1873, and remained a member until his decease in 1883. At the time of his death he was considered the oldest Fox-Terrier breeder in England. He started his strain at Oxford when he was eighteen, and more than fifty years afterwards had pedigrees that he could trace from the time he began to breed Fox-Terriers. Mr. Russell's Terriers in working condition did not scale more than 15lb., some even less, and between forty and fifty years ago they formed a very distinct type. He judged Fox-Terriers at the Kennel Club Show in the Crystal Palace in June, 1874."

By advertising it is possible one might obtain in Devonshire or Cornwall Terriers that could be traced back to those of the hunting parson of the West Country, but it was scarcely the custom in those far-off days for those who kept Terriers

F

for the sport they afforded rather than for the pleasure of
seeing them in a show-ring, to keep any strict account of
pedigrees, and on that account there might be some little
difficulty in establishing their claims to being considered the
Simon-pure article. At any rate, the strain was such a
notable one that it deserves to be perpetuated and carefully
perpetuated.

Sporting and Other Qualities.

All that has been said in respect of the temperament,
&c., of the Smooth variety may be truthfully said of the
Wire-Haired. The best of these Terriers are excellent
companions, and game to a fault. They are very
hard-bitten, yet they may be trained to almost any kind
of work of which a dog of the size is capable. By some
it is not infrequently sought to show that, while the Smooth-
Haired variety is the racier and showier-looking, the
Wire-Haired is the gamer. In practice, however, the latter
has been proved to have no foundation in fact. This,
however, may be stated with considerable truth, that
a really good Wire-Haired, possessing the requisite hard
outer coat and the soft, close inner one, will withstand cold
and exposure to wet better than the Smooth. As with the
Smooth so with the Wire-Haired Terrier, there has been
a disposition on the part of breeders to favour a smaller
type of dog ; and if the breed is really to maintain its status
as one fitted to go to earth, the modification is not only
desirable, but eminently necessary. No day is too long for
a Terrier of the right sort.

Outside the somewhat restricted area of the fancy, as
well as within its pale, are to be found occasionally
strains of first-class working dogs. Mr. Francis
Redmond, the late Mr. J. A. Doyle, and Mr. R. Vicary
(to whose exertions in respect of the Smooths we owe so
much as regards coats) are names that readily recur in
connection therewith. Still, it is scarcely to be expected that

the average owner is going to run the risk of entering, say,
a £200 dog to fox, otter, or badger.   There are, however,
others who breed a certain class of Terrier for the purpose.
Such was the Sealyham Terrier identified with the name of
the late Capt. Edwardes; while others scarcely less noteworthy are those that Mr. Heinemann, Mr. Cowley, and Mr.
Schreiber have familiarised us with.   Similarly, there are
many huntsmen who have Fox-Terriers that are every bit
as game as were their remote progenitors.   With these,
handsome is that handsome does.

Description of the Breed.

So far as this is concerned, there is little to be said
as the description of the Smooth will apply in every particular save that of coat to the Wire-Haired.

STANDARD OF POINTS.

Head and Ears	15
Neck	5
Shoulders and Chest	15
Back and Loin	10
Hindquarters	5
Stern	5
Legs and Feet	20
Coat	10
Symmetry, Size, and Character	15
Total	100

Disqualifying Points.

In either the Smooth- or the Wire-Haired variety the following
defects should disqualify :

Nose, white, cherry, or spotted to a considerable extent with
either of these colours.

Ears, prick, tulip, or rose.

Mouth much undershot or much overshot.

F 2

THE MALTESE TERRIER.

THOUGH no longer regarded as a Terrier by the powers that be, this little silky toy-dog was for many years so classed, and in a popular work on the group many people would naturally look for some information concerning it. Suffice it to say that in 1903 the Kennel Club decided that this beautiful variety that had been kept as a pet by ladies from the time of the ancient Greeks and Romans was henceforth to be classed as the " Maltese Dog."   Still, long ere the Kennel Club had made such an alteration, Stonehenge and several others had suggested that it had none of the " properties of the Terrier tribe," though even that well-informed writer was strangely inconsistent, as he also wrote of it as a " beautiful little Skye Terrier in miniature."

As to the advisability of removing this Toy from the list of Terriers, we are not concerned here.   The Kennel Club no doubt had excellent reasons for arriving at such a decision, and we may take it that it was not done until its status as regards the Terrier group had been thoroughly considered.

THE MINIATURE BLACK-AND-TAN TERRIER.

Make and Shape.

POPULARLY this Toy Terrier is supposed to be a pocket edition of the Manchester Terrier elsewhere described. It is, however, rarely indeed that one comes across a specimen that with truth may be so designated. As is the case with Toys generally, it is of a delicate constitution, and it would be inadvisable ever to mete out to it the treatment given to the larger dog. Coddling, on the other hand, is equally to be condemned. At one time it was customary to see apple-headed, almost hairless monstrosities passing as Toy Black-and-Tan Terriers; but the breeder has changed all that, and the smart little dog has been very much improved of late with the exception of the ears.

Still, even as regards the delicacy of constitution referred to, there is by no means unanimity of opinion. One of the best-known breeders of these Toys thus writes : " The breeding is attended with so little trouble, and, notwithstanding their accredited delicacy, with so little risk, that it is a perpetual wonder to me that there should be so few recruits to the fancy. In the first place, they are so essentially house-pets that a garden can be dispensed with; even the London back yard is not an absolute necessity; so that ladies whose home is in flat-land need not be debarred from the pleasure and profit of breeding these—the smartest and prettiest of Toy dogs."

Craze for the Small.

In this breed as in others there is a craze shown for the very small, and all sorts of artifices have been resorted to in order to achieve this object.   Opinions differ as to the best way of mating these dogs.   One breeder known to the writer always bred from the smallest Toy-bred bitch that could be procured, and mated her, the first time she was available, with a small sire of, say, two years.   There is, however, so much risk in such a method of procedure that we should hesitate to recommend it.   Far better would it be to select a medium-sized bitch coming of a small strain and mate her, the second time she was in season, to a much older dog that was also small and came of a small stock.

**One of Mrs. Whaley's Miniature Black-and-Tan Terriers—
Champion Coquette.**

Naturally, where very miniature dogs are concerned there is plenty of room for diversity of opinion as regards the best method of breeding them.   We have already voiced our own opinion on the matter; and we will now quote that of a breeder whose views, if not widely different from our own, are sufficiently so to be worth giving.   Probably in the mean between the two will lie the path for the novice to choose. At any rate, there is, as we have often said, nothing hard-and-fast in respect of Nature's laws, and a plan that may prove a failure at one period may at another turn out an unqualified success.   The breeder referred to states that as regards a sire, one should be chosen when in his prime, which is about the age of two years, before he begins to

" sport the grey " ; and as the rage for smallness unhappily still continues, the surest way of obtaining diminutive puppies is to mate him with a Toy-bred (not Manchester-bred) bitch even smaller than himself, and to breed at the first heat. Then, with regard to the brood bitch, she states that there is no necessity to keep a large brood bitch, believing that a small, handsome specimen is as capable of breeding as a large, ugly one.

Special Management.

Naturally such an atom of dog-flesh as the Miniature Black-and-Tan Terrier needs to be treated carefully.   It should be kept indoors during winter and allowed to obtain the requisite exercise by running after a ball.   It should also have a tray of earth or sanitary sawdust provided.   This could be stood in an out-of-the-way place in the scullery, and the dog allowed access thereto.   In summer the dog is all the better for exercise outside, and for living a more or less outdoor life : the coat then is so much thicker and better in every way.   Should a bitch be bred from in winter the puppies must not be allowed outside.   They will soon learn to resort to the tray of earth or what not, and the risk of losing them from cold is minimised.

The Coat Trouble.

One of the chief things that the breeder of these dogs has to contend against is lack of coat, and it is not at all unusual to find specimens of the breed that might be Hairless dogs for all the coat they possess.   From the first it should be encouraged by gentle brushing and stimulants—a little lanolin, for instance, applied to the coat and well rubbed in once or twice a week.   The puppies must also be judiciously fed ; some fanciers, in their endeavours to keep the puppies small, practically half-starve them, and in such a case is there any wonder that the coat is scanty and bare ? We know of one successful breeder of these Toys who pinned

her faith as regards coat production to allowing the dog
a certain amount of cooked fat meat, of course taking care
that this was not overdone.

Interesting " Sports."

In this breed one meets with two interesting sports in the
Blue Paul and the Blue-and-Tan. By some these are dignified
by the name of varieties, but they have no claim to be so
considered. Moreover, in the old days when the " faking "
of these Terriers was made almost a fine art, they were
occasionally painted the requisite shade of blue.

**Mrs. Whaley's Miniature Black-and-Tan Terrier
Glenartney Dick.**

There are also other colour sports—Liver-and-Tan—but
these are rarer still than the Blue-and-Tan. Years ago there
were one or two breeders who had a strain of Blue-and-Tan
Toy Terriers, and if we mistake not the Countess of Cotten-
ham was among the number. Fanciers and breeders do not
appear to view with favour these colour-sports, and are apt
to regard them as " mismarked specimens." How far it
is desirable to perpetuate such sports is quite another matter.
One breeder we know, who makes Blue-and-Tans a speciality,
states that it is quite easy to breed them : a Blue-and-Tan
mated with a Black-and-Tan will invariably throw blue
puppies. It is therefore quite easy to form a strain.
Further, she states that the Blue-and-Tan are quite as hardy

as the Black-and-Tan. Except that the tan is a little paler—lemon, in fact—and the hair somewhat softer in texture, the markings of the Blue-and-Tan follow those of the Black-and-Tan.

House-dog Qualities, &c.

For giving the alarm these little dogs are excellent in a house, where they are readily accommodated in a nicely-lined basket or one that contains a Petanelle rug. They should also appeal to those who, not having the accommodation to breed any of the larger Terriers, are yet able to offer a corner in a room to a mother and her whelps.

Points.

These are practically identical with those given in connection with the larger dog; but the ear-carriage is nothing like so constant in the small as in the large breed, and not a few breeders are averse to having widely different types of ears in the two varieties.

THE OLD ENGLISH TERRIER.

As this erstwhile breed has no longer any standing as such, and has, moreover, been expurgated from the list of varieties acknowledged by the Kennel Club authorities, it necessarily is not included in this work. Under the Welsh Terrier the reader will find discussed the reason for its non-recognition by the powers that be—namely, a lack of fixity of type. At one time it looked as if this dog would be a serious competitor to the Welsh Terrier, and though it was projected upon the doggy firmament with all the brilliance of the rocket, it came down like the proverbial stick.

For all that it is only fair to state that long before show-habitués were familiarised with the dog that is now known as a Welsh Terrier, there existed in many parts of England a wire-haired Black-and-Tan Terrier. Moreover, the Kennel Club at one time actually classified these black-and-tan hard-coated Terriers as " Welsh or Old English Wire-haired Black-and-Tan Terriers." In the districts of the North there certainly existed such a dog as Wales claims as its Terrier, but whether the one or the other had prior claims to being considered *the* variety it is not possible to say. In most natural history subjects priority of nomenclature attaches to the older name; but he would be a bold man indeed who asserted that before the black-and-tan Terrier, subsequently named the Old English Terrier was, the Welsh Terrier was, or *vice versa*; and as such we must leave the subject with all its elements of doubt.

Anyhow, the Old English Terrier, as a variety of British dogs, was short-lived, and if the somewhat discordant elements out of which the majority of the specimens seen were evolved could have been separated they would have revealed an extraordinary composition. Some approached the Airedale Terrier, and others the Fox-Terrier with a dash of Manchester, &c. Little wonder, therefore, that a breed so lacking in cohesion had to go, and no one seemed particularly sorry when the Old English Terrier as a breed farce was no longer enacted.

THE WELSH TERRIER.

Original Types.

" GALLANT little Wales " can boast a Terrier that is quite
as full of " go " and pluck as are the inhabitants of the
Principality. It is, however, a variety that has had a somewhat chequered career, and from the first it was unfortunate
in getting such scant treatment at shows when it was classified
with Old English Black-and-Tan Terriers. If we look back
a little into history we shall find that black-and-tan was the
colour of the first Terrier of which we have any trustworthy
description, and the probability, therefore, is that even
before the Fox-Terrier, as we now know it, existed there
was as an assistant to hounds a Terrier approximating in type
to the little dog under discussion. Though in England the
breed as it originally existed may have been, and probably
was, absorbed in the making of others, it is possible that the
Welshman preferred to keep the Terrier in the state in which
it existed. At any rate, in various centres—in Carnarvonshire
in particular—this Terrier had a considerable vogue, even
though dog shows had not begun to make their influence
felt. Moreover, it is evident that more than ordinary care
was taken with the breeding of the dog, as trustworthy pedigrees exist that go back more than half a century. As a
show dog with a classification its career is a comparatively
short one, dating back less than a quarter of a century. In
those days everyone who had some sort of a black-and-
tan wire-haired Terrier imagined that he had a Welsh
Terrier, and, as a consequence, there was not in those early
exhibits the uniformity of type that existed a little later, and
exists still more to-day. Doubtless, too, it was this that
caused the late Mr. Hugh Dalziel to write them down as a

" scratch pack "—a description that rankled in the breast of many a fancier of the real article. Another circumstance that at the time tended to retard the progress of the breed was the introduction of a more or less mongrelised animal in the Old English Terrier, a dog that would not breed true to type.

In the early days of the Welsh Terrier there was a good

A Champion Welsh Terrier of Mr. W. S. Glynn's famous strain—
Brynhir Ballad.

deal of friendly rivalry shown between the Welshmen who claimed purity of descent for their national dog and the Englishmen in the North. The latter certainly owned some excellent dogs, and whether they were the products of the Principality or just a local strain of Terrier that had proved worth breeding, they more than held their own in open competition with the best. It is, moreover, a notorious fact that dogs have been shown and won honours alike as Welsh Terriers and as Old English Terriers. Of the fanciers who distinguished themselves with these Terriers in the early days of the fancy mention should be made of Mr. W. S. Glynn (the principal breeder at the present day), Colonel Savage, Mr. A. Maxwell, Mr. W. J. M. Herbert, Mr. W. A. Drew, Mr. E. Buckley, Mr. Hayward Field, Mr. C. H. Beck, Mr. W. E. Alcock, Dr. Edwardes Ker, Mr. W. C. Whiskin, and Mr. W. C. Roberts.

Recommendations.

Originally a Kennel Terrier—just as were the progenitors of our modern Fox-Terriers—and kept as an assistant to hounds, both those employed in hunting the fox and the otter, the variety possesses just that characteristic gameness that one naturally looks for in such a dog. Shows in the case of the Welsh Terrier have certainly not dulled its wits nor damped its courage, for the present-day dog is as keen as were any of its ancestors of half a century since. As a companion for either town or country the Welsh Terrier may be described as the best of " pals " and the most alert of guards in a house. Having no coat readily to show signs of soiling, the variety may be kept even in the smokiest of towns, where a white breed is almost out of the question. Game though the dog is, there is nothing headstrong or quarrelsome about it : on the contrary, it is one of the best-mannered of all the Terriers, and on this account alone its popularity should be still further assured. On land or in the water, it matters not what is required of the dog in reason he is capable of performing the task, and in nine times out of ten with credit. Even the housewife not generally partial to dogs has a good word for " Taffy," for he has no long coat to lick up the mud and is of a size that is not obtrusive when kept indoors as " one of the family."

As a Show Dog.

In connection with the Welsh Terrier from the show point of view entirely, there are drawbacks that the novice cannot afford to ignore. There is no gainsaying the fact that the breed is one that has to be trimmed very carefully. Any little bungling will either end in the dog's being disqualified or put back. What has been said in respect of the preparation of the Airedale Terrier holds good to a certain extent of this breed. We say "to a certain extent" advisedly, for the variety as regards coat has been immensely improved, and there is therefore not the need of trimming to the extent formerly necessary. The prospective exhibitor not having had any initiatory lessons in the art of preparing dogs for show would be well advised to get an expert to put him in the way. Even then he will not find it an easy task to touch up the head of a Welsh Terrier in the way beloved of those who specialise in this breed. There are some specimens that require very little extra preparation, but this cannot be said of the majority.

From the first there has been little to complain of in the jackets of this breed, though there is still room for a smaller and more shapely ear, a better muzzle and front, a shorter body and more powerful quarters, and smaller and more compact feet. There is a tendency towards producing a bigger dog, and one that approaches the Fox-Terrier in head properties; but this is a mistake, as the head of a Welsh Terrier should be relatively shorter than that of the Fox-Terrier.

Choosing a Puppy.

Unless it is absolutely necessary that a choice should be made while the puppies are with the dam, we would strongly advise that the selection be postponed until the six months. By that time the coat texture and colour may be fore-shadowed with more or less certainty; whereas with very young puppies it is not at all uncommon for the colour to be quite different from what one sees on an adult dog; while the texture is often more puzzling still. As the description furnished specifically states the dog should be black-and-tan, or black, grizzle and tan, in colour; but just as the Airedale Terrier when young looks like a smooth Black-and-Tan Terrier, so the Welsh Terrier not infrequently shows only the tan, the black, or the black and grizzle filling in afterwards. We have known at least one or two instances where litters in which appeared all-tan dogs were viewed with suspicion, and such mismarked specimens (as the owners thought) would have been summarily got rid of had not an experienced Welsh fancier and breeder advised their being kept for a time. His advice proved sound, as the " tan " puppies in each case turned out excellent specimens.

A defect, though not a fatal one, with Welsh Terriers is a little white on chest; but specimens so marked must not be too seriously regarded. In many breeds—self-coloured ones especially—there is a tendency in certain individuals for white hairs to be produced there; but when only a few hairs (not a patch) are found, say, on a puppy, the chances are that they will moult out as the adult stage is assumed. Moreover, no judge would heavily penalise an otherwise typical dog for a comparatively slight defect. If in combination with the promise of a good jacket there are a long head, small V-shaped drop ears, powerful jaw, and dark eye, straight, well-boned forelegs, and a short body, then the prospective purchaser has a very excellent chance of possessing a thoroughly representative specimen when it is full grown.

Description of the Breed.

A very excellent club by which the interests of this Terrier are well safeguarded exists, and the description here given is the one for which it is responsible :—

Head.—The skull should be flat, and rather wider between the ears than that of the Wire-Haired Fox-Terrier. The jaw should be powerful, clean cut, rather deeper, and more punishing, giving the head a more masculine appearance than that usually seen on a Fox-Terrier. Stop not too defined, fair length from stop to end of nose, the latter being black.

Ears.—The ear should be V-shaped, small, not too thin, set on fairly high, carried forward and close to the cheek.

Eyes.—The eyes should be small, not being too deeply set in or protruding out of skull, of a dark hazel colour, expressive and indicating abundant pluck.

Neck.—The neck should be of moderate length and thickness, slightly arched, and sloping gracefully into the shoulders.

Body.—The back should be short and well ribbed-up, the loin strong and of good depth, and the chest moderately wide. The shoulders should be long, sloping, and well set back. The hindquarters should be strong, thighs muscular and of good length, with the hocks moderately straight, well let down, and with a fair amount of bone. The stern should be set on moderately high, but not too gaily carried.

Legs and Feet.—The legs should be straight and muscular, possessing fair amount of bone, with upright and powerful pasterns. The feet should be small, round, and cat-like.

Coat.—The coat should be wiry, hard, very close, and abundant.

Colour.—The colour should be black-and-tan, or black-grizzle-and-tan, free from black pencilling on toes.

Size.—The height at shoulder should be 15in. for dogs, bitches proportionately less. Twenty pounds shall be considered a fair average weight in working condition, but this may vary a pound or so either way.

STANDARD OF EXCELLENCE.

Head	20
Ears and Eyes	10
Neck and Shoulders	5
Body, Ribs, and Hindquarters	15
Coat	25
Legs and Feet	10
Tail and Carriage of Same	5
General Appearance	10
Total	**100**

THE YORKSHIRE TERRIER.

A Working Man's Creation.

UNIVERSALLY admired as this distinctive little Toy Terrier is for the wealth and beauty of its coat, yet it is impossible for anyone having any practical knowledge of dogs generally to view it without feeling that he is looking upon a very artificial production; but one thing is certain: the breed is one for which we are entirely indebted to the patience and care of the working man. From very unpromising material that he found ready to hand he produced the dog that we know to-day as the Yorkshire Terrier, but which prior to 1886, when the Kennel Club acknowledged the name, was known as " Rough and Broken-Coated," " Broken-Haired Scotch and Yorkshire Terriers," and " Rough Toy Terriers." The word " Scotch " had doubtless some reference to one of the constituents employed in the " manufacture " of the breed—the Paisley or the Skye Terrier; but in any case the most appropriate name is the one it now bears, for the county of broad acres was its undoubted birthplace. Indeed, we may go farther and say that to the factory operatives of Bradford, Huddersfield, and Halifax chiefly belongs the credit, if not of actually producing, certainly of perfecting, this elegant Toy Terrier. These men waxed very enthusiastic over their Terriers, and shows were arranged and a spirit of friendly rivalry engendered that soon made for gradual improvements in the breed.

At no period in its history has the Yorkshire Terrier been other than a breed for the specialist, and though at varying times in its career it has attained a fair measure of public favour, it has never been popular in the true sense of that term. The very conditions under which it must be kept, and the skill and labour required to bring it to perfection as a show dog have been retarding factors. Many a lady seeing the dog at a show has been enamoured with its attractive coat, and has purchased it perhaps, only to find that it was one thing to buy a dog with such a coat and another to keep it in the condition that first attracted her.

Casually to look at the Yorkshire Terrier is to put it down as a more or less useless breed—a dog, in fact, that

A Typical Show Yorkshire Terrier.

is valued only for its ornamental qualities. Still, small though it be, and fragile in appearance, yet it is capable of rendering a good account of itself against a rat; while in the house it is a smart, alert, active house-dog. Ladies are nowadays the most skilful fanciers of Yorkshire Terriers, and the names of several are writ large in the scroll of fame. Mrs. Foster, Mrs. Troughear, and the Mesdames Walton and Beard are a quartet whose successes have been remarkable. One thing, however, is certain, the breed is one that requires not only considerable knowledge on the part of the fancier, but that entails plenty of patience and labour to show it in perfection of coat.

Housing.

The show Yorkshire Terrier has of necessity to lead an entirely artificial life. Its kennel must be kept indoors, and, except for a run out now and again for natural purposes, it must be more or less a prisoner. Nor must it frolic and gambol with other dogs. Makers of kennel appliances now sell kennels specially adapted to the life the dog has to lead, modelled, no doubt, on those more primitive appliances that the Yorkshire fanciers employed when the breed was in the making. Except in very fine weather and most favourable conditions under foot, the dog cannot be allowed outside, as to do so would be fatal to its chances in the show-ring. Even at shows it cannot be benched like hardy Terriers, but has to be looked at through the bars of the daintily-decorated cages specially provided for its requirements. At shows, too, the fitments of such cages are suggestive of the daily life the dog has to lead. Bedding material as ordinarily understood—straw, hay, and the like—it must have none of, or the coat would be injured. A cushion of some kind, and preferably one stuffed with a material that does not readily harbour dust, must be provided, and this kept well beaten and periodically changed. As there are many days on which a Yorkshire Terrier would not be allowed outside even for natural purposes, it is customary to provide in a corner of the apartment in which the dog's kennel is placed some sanitary sawdust or a little straw to which it can have access.

There are short-coated specimens which are not required for show purposes, and these need not, of course, lead such a life as those required for show. Being active little animals they may be kept just on the lines of any other small pet dog, though it is not advisable even for these to go out during bad weather. At such times they may be exercised indoors by means of a ball or similar plaything. Nor need a cage be provided for them. During the day they may sleep about the house, and at night a dog-basket and a Petanelle or other rug will provide them with all the covering they need. These short-coated Yorkshires are excellent house-dogs—alert, active, and first-rate companions.

The Show Dog Considered.

The show preparation of the Yorkshire Terrier is a big and very special business, and not one dog-fancier in a thousand is capable of undertaking it. Moreover, it is a lengthy business. First, we will assume that the fancier has purchased a comparatively young puppy of first-class strain—one whose parents, grandparents, and great-grandparents at least have, in their turn, produced long-coated specimens. It is quite useless to attempt to produce a long coat from a Yorkshire whose ancestors have never been distinguished for such characteristics. Before, however, we make any attempt to deal with the method of coat-growing adopted, it will be well to refer to a peculiarity of the breed as regards puppies. When born, and for some considerable time after, Yorkshire Terriers are about as unlike the adult animal as anything well could be— they are black and tan, or perhaps it would be more correct to say that they are black, with tanned muzzle and feet. The change from this colour to the one characteristic of the variety is most gradual, the age at which it commences varying with strains and individuals. Some coats show a slight change at the third month, while others do not perceptibly change until from the sixth to the twelfth month. Still, long before the latter period is reached, it is necessary to commence the special grooming and coat stimulation that are necessary. Once a day the coat must be brushed, using for the purpose one of the special brushes sold by dealers in fanciers' appliances. Naturally, in the case of a very young dog, the grooming must not be such as is likely to cause the skin any irritation. Each week it is advisable thoroughly to rub in a little lanolin or sweet oil and paraffin

(two parts of the former to one of the latter). The action
of the stimulant must be carefully studied. The greasy compound must not be too lavishly applied, or harm rather than
good will result. At the end of a month from the date of
the first application of the fat (which may very well be commenced at about the end of the third month) the puppy may
be washed and very carefully dried, having regard to the
future " lay" of the coat. The hair, which is parted down
the centre, must not be treated as one would in washing a
hardy Terrier, but cleansed rather by means of a sponge, with
as little disturbance to the coat as possible. This cleansing
process would be facilitated by using one of the shampoo
washes now so much in vogue, and with less risk than
attaches to ordinary soap. Still, the skin condition must
be the guide; if it is at all irritable no soap should be
used, or anything likely to intensify the trouble. The
drying is no less important than the washing, and
this also must be undertaken with due regard to the
ultimate lay of the coat. Warm towels and brushes should
be employed, and on no account must the puppy be returned
to its kennel until the coat is properly dry. When it is
observed that the coat is both lengthening and increasing in
thickness a stronger stimulant may be tried, and the hind
feet encased in leather shoes, so as to prevent the
dog from scratching. Such may take the following
form : Olive oil, 3oz. ; castor oil, 3oz. ; palm oil,
1oz. ; vaseline, 1oz. ; tincture of cantharides, 1dr. ; oil of
rosemary, 1dr. Mix the first two together, and add the rest
while simmering over a fire. Or the sweet oil and paraffin
above referred to may be employed. Some fanciers
use the stimulant once a week ; others much oftener, according to its action upon the skin. Tincture of cantharides
sometimes causes irritation ; in that case it should at once
be stopped. The stimulant must be applied to moustache
and fall as well as to the body proper ; and when the coat
is sufficiently long to justify its being done, the " fall " (as
the long hair covering the face is termed by fanciers)

should be plaited and tied up over the head with ribbon. The combing and brushing must be regularly done (a brush for the purpose is sold by all dog-appliance manufacturers), but care must be taken not to break the coat in any way. For that reason the greasy compounds referred to must be carefully put on—just a little in the palm of the hand, and rubbed in with the lay of the coat. It will be gathered from this that the show Yorkshire is by no means easy to produce, even given the

Brush for Yorkshire Terriers and other long-coated Toys.

requisite " blood " to start with. Still, now that the fancy are inclined to recognise a coat of less length than was formerly held imperative, it looks as if better times were in store for this Toy dog.

Feeding.

Even in this particular the Yorkshire Terrier differs from the majority of its congeners, as anything calculated to overheat the blood would be fatal to the dog's chances of growing the requisite coat. Well-cooked rice, either mixed with a little gravy or in the form of the familiar milk pudding as prepared for children; a little fish (this tends to give lustre to the coat); well-cooked vegetables, but not many potatoes, covered with gravy; stale brown bread similarly treated; Pet-dog biscuits; cooked tripe; a little plain pudding, as served to young children; and very occasionally some finely-minced raw beef (by way of a tonic) are all foods that may be

recommended for these little dogs. When the coat begins to
" break " the dog will be benefited by giving now and
again a little fat meat. This is contrary to the generally
accepted notion; but if it can be taken without causing any
disturbance, it will have a beneficial effect upon the coat.
Here, again, the owner will have to use judgment, and
must carefully watch the individual dog. Again, as this
Toy dog is allowed but little or no exercise as usually understood, the bowels must be carefully regulated by means of a
judicious dietary.

Breeding Hints.

As will be seen by the description that follows, Yorkshire Terriers weigh from 5lb. and under to 7lb. and over.
Still, with this as with most other Toys the craze is for the
very small, and specimens of 2lb. weight have been produced; while 4lb. to 4½lb. Yorkshires have been common
enough. Even these " weighty " dogs are not best calculated to make ideal brood bitches, as there would be not a
little risk to them at whelping time. A medium-sized well-
bred young bitch, coming of a small strain, mated to a suitable old sire, also of a small strain, or an old bitch
mated to a young sire, would be far better. The puppies of
this variety have to be docked, about half the tail being
removed. Formerly, too, it was the fashion to crop the
Yorkshire Terrier, though the cruel practice has been discontinued for some years.

Other Colours.

There has been a tendency shown of late to make a
variety of what are really badly-coloured specimens of the
breed. This, we think, is a mistake. A very similar thing
has been done with several other varieties, and anything
but good has resulted from the innovation. The so-called
" Silvers " we think should not be encouraged by those
having the best interests of the breed at heart.

Description.

Alike in the North and the South this Terrier has clubs to protect its interests, and the description that follows is one drawn up by the Yorkshire Terrier Club :—

General Appearance.—The general appearance should be that of a long-coated pet-dog, the coat hanging quite straight and evenly down each side, a parting extending from the nose to the end of the tail. The animal should be very compact and neat, the carriage being very sprightly. Although the frame is hidden beneath a mantle of hair, the general outline should be such as to suggest the existence of a vigorous and well-proportioned body.

Head.—This should be rather small and flat, not too prominent or round in the skull, nor too long in the muzzle, with a perfectly black nose. The fall on the head should be very long and of a rich golden tan, deeper in colour at the sides of the head about the ear roots and on the muzzle, where it should be very long. The hair on the chest should be a rich bright tan. On no account must the tan on the head extend on to the neck; nor must there be any sooty or dark hairs intermingled with any of the tan.

Eyes.—Medium, dark, and sparkling, having a sharp, intelligent expression, and placed so as to look directly forward. They should not be prominent, and the edge of the eyelids should be dark.

Ears.—These should be small, V-shaped, and carried semi-erect or erect, covered with short hair, the colour being of a deep rich tan.

Mouth.—Perfectly even, with teeth as sound as possible. An animal having lost any teeth through accident is not a fault, providing the jaws are even.

Body.—Very compact, with a good loin, and level on top of the back.

Coat.—The hair on the body should be as long as possible, and perfectly straight (not wavy), glossy like silk, and of a fine silky texture. Colour a dark steel-blue (not a silver-blue) extending from the occiput to the root of the tail, and on no account mingled with fawn, bronze, or dark hairs.

Legs.—Quite straight, and well covered with hair of a rich golden tan a few shades lighter at the ends than at the roots, not extending higher on the fore legs than the elbow, nor on the hind legs than the stifle.

Feet.—As round as possible, and the toe-nails black.

Tail.—Docked to medium length; with plenty of hair, darker blue in colour than the rest of the body, especially at the end of the tail, and carried a little higher than the level of the back.

Tan.—All tan hair should be darker at the roots than in the middle, shading to a still lighter tan at the tips.

Weight.—Divided into three classes : 5lb. and under; 7lb. and under, but over 5lb. ; and over 7lb.

STANDARD OF POINTS.

Quantity and Length of Coat	15
Quality and Texture of Coat	10
Richness of Tan on Head and Legs ...	15
Colour of Hair on Body	15
Head	10
Eyes	5
Ears	5
Legs and Feet	5
Tail Carriage	5
Mouth	5
Formation and General Appearance ...	10
Total	100

DIVISION II.

Scotch and Irish Terriers.

Section and Field of Vision.

Scotch and Irish Terriers.

THE CLYDESDALE TERRIER.

A Little-known Breed.

However much we may feel disposed to wax enthusiastic over this essentially Scottish variety, there is no denying its scarcity or the fact that it is a breed which is rapidly becoming decadent. Nor is the reason far to seek when one considers how notoriously difficult it is to keep the dog in anything like show condition for any length of time. Still, all this is to be deplored, for the breed received the hall-mark of variety nearly thirty years ago. Prior to that, however, it was classified among " Broken-Haired Scotch Terriers." As is the case with many another Terrier, the Clydesdale has received several names—Silkie, Paisley, and Glasgow Terrier having all been bestowed upon it. The first was in reference to its coat, and the last two speak for themselves. Like the Yorkshire Terrier, which sprang therefrom, the Clydesdale Terrier was at one time principally a working-man's breed—a character, moreover, that it retains practically to the present day.

Writers upon dogs have often endeavoured to trace the origin of this long-coated pet-dog, though it must be confessed that, as is the case with the older breeds generally, nothing very definite has been arrived at. When, however, the dog is viewed critically it is fairly easy to see that the Clydesdale and the Skye were produced from a common stock. There are, of course, differences observable between

B

them which will be duly considered; but the general appearance of the two varieties betokens a common origin.

Compared with the Skye.

If anyone will take the trouble to note carefully two typical specimens of the breeds between which a comparison is instituted, he will see that the Clydesdale Terrier is smaller, silkier as to coat, more compact as to body, taller, and shows a more profuse ear-feathering than its congener

A Typical Clydesdale Terrier.

the Skye. Viewed casually, however, these differences are not noticeable, and we have often heard the two breeds confused by novices at shows. Moreover, too, in the old days of dog shows the Skye and the Clydesdale were pitted against one another as "Broken-Haired Scotch Terriers," the Silkie often proving too many for the Skye, and jealousy between the two sections of the fancy was rife.

Eventually the Clydesdale partisans were strong enough to demand a separate classification, and this was accorded in 1885. From that time onward until now the breeds have been kept distinct.

As a Show Dog.

On account of the difficulties that beset the show preparation of this breed, it must be classed, like the Yorkshire Terrier, as fit only for a specialist and destined to pass the greater part of its life indoors. The washing, grooming, and coat-stimulation incidental to the Yorkshire Terrier, the care of the coat from puppyhood to maturity, the special dietary, kennelling, and bedding, apply equally to this variety. The fancier, therefore, who essays to take up this breed with a view to exhibiting it will find that to put the dog down in condition is no light task. It is not proposed here to enter into the details necessary therefor, as they will be found fully set out under the Yorkshire Terrier in " English and Welsh Terriers " ; while under the Skye Terrier in the present work will be found other suggestions that might be profitably adopted. There is, however, one matter, unsavoury though it may be, that should be mentioned in connection with this breed—namely, the dyeing that is practised by the unscrupulous with a view to deceive. The novice, therefore, who essays to purchase without enlisting any assistance should make sure that the beautiful steel-blue or even the golden tan has not been produced artificially.

As a Companion.

Those who have had the opportunity of testing the capabilities of these beautiful pet-dogs speak very highly with regard to their qualities in this direction. Still, we cannot help thinking that, by reason of the conditions under which these dogs have to be kept, if they are to have a typical coat such qualities would necessarily be largely discounted, as except in very fine weather the dogs would be restricted to the house and curtilage. As is the case with

the Skye Terrier, the Clydesdale is a fairly robust variety
and an excellent and alert house-dog. For ladies it would
make an ideal companion, and we have often wondered why
the breed has not more seriously attracted their attention.
Some of its more enthusiastic admirers have often written
and spoken of its abilities as a vermin dog; but, generally
speaking, it can only be regarded as a purely ornamental
breed.

Clubs and Description.

From time to time specialist clubs to foster the interests
of the " Silkie " have arisen; but they have not been destined
to a very long life. The Skye and Clydesdale Terrier Club,
however, exists, and is doubtless doing good work. At any
rate, it has issued a description of the breed as follows :—

General Appearance.—A long, low, level dog with heavily
fringed, erect ears, and a long coat like the finest silk or spun
glass, which hangs quite straight and evenly down each side, a
parting extending from the nose to the root of the tail.

Head.—Fairly long, skull flat, and very narrow between the
ears, gradually widening towards the eyes and tapering very
slightly to the nose, which must be black. The jaws strong and the
teeth level.

Eyes.—Medium in size, dark in colour, not prominent, but having
a sharp, Terrier-like expression. Eyelids black.

Ears.—Small, set very high on the top of the head, carried perfectly erect, and covered with long, silky hair, hanging in a heavy
fringe down the sides of the head.

Body.—Long, deep in chest, well ribbed up, the back being
perfectly level.

Tail.—Perfectly straight, carried almost level with the back,
and heavily feathered.

Legs.—As short and straight as possible, well set under the body,
and entirely covered with silky hair. Feet round and cat-like.

Coat.—As long and straight as possible, free from all trace of curl or waviness; very glossy and silky in texture, with an entire absence of undercoat.

Colour.—A level bright steel blue, extending from the back of the head to the root of the tail, and on no account intermingled with any fawn, light, or dark hairs. The head, legs, and feet should be a clear, bright, golden tan, free from grey, sooty, or dark hairs. The tail should be very dark blue or black.

SCALE OF POINTS.

Texture of Coat	25
Colour	25
Head	10
Ears	10
Tail	10
Body	10
Legs and Feet	10
Total	100

THE DANDIE DINMONT TERRIER.

Immortalised by Scott.

THOUGH the name Dandie Dinmont as applied to this
Terrier could only have been a creation after 1814, the
year in which Sir Walter Scott's "Guy Mannering" first
saw the light, yet the dog itself existed at a period long
anterior to this. That, too, it was a game Terrier admits
of little doubt : the very purposes for which it was used
are sufficient to warrant the assumption. Like many another
hardy Terrier associated with Scotland or the Border
Counties, it was in the hands of families of gipsies who
would not for one moment have tolerated anything incapable
of rendering a good account of itself when pitted against
the polecats and other equally determined members of the
Weasel group that were fairly common in those days; while
it also had to do duty on occasion against still larger
"vermin," and frequently to act as assistant to the gun.

These Terriers are a kind of first-cousin to the Bedlington
Terrier, whose origin and uses were dealt with in "English
and Welsh Terriers," and were kept and prized by men with
similar sporting instincts. This is seen alike as regards the
topknot and the colour, though the former has been "cultivated" and is a product of recent years rather than a
characteristic of the dog prior to its present name being
applied. If we are to place credence in historical records,
the Terrier we now know as Dandie Dinmont was kept
and valued by one "Piper" Allan of Bellingham as long
ago as 1704. He was but one of many belonging to the
nomadic tribe whose name history has handed down to
us in connection with this game Terrier. Mr. Charles
Cook, in his excellent monograph of the breed published

in 1885, records facts that go unmistakably to show that these Allans of Holystone possessed a particularly game strain of Terrier to which neither polecat, otter, fox, nor badger, if report speaks truly, came amiss. The first Allan of which we have record is "Piper," so named from the fact that he tramped the countryside with his bagpipes. That the strain of Terrier associated with this itinerant musician must have been an exceptional one we deduce

Type of Dandie Dinmont Terrier—Mrs. Peel Hewitt's Champion Tommy Atkins.

from the fact that he was offered by a nobleman a homestead in exchange for a particular specimen, an offer that was refused. Enthusiasts in the breed have ever sought to show that the Dandie Dinmont Terrier was descended from Piper Allan's famous dogs. There is, however, nothing to point the way, and the chances are that in those days very little was done to preserve in an unbroken line anything like purity of descent. Much, therefore, as we should like to establish his claim, we are unable

to do so from the fact that so many links in the chain
are wanting.   We therefore perforce take up the Terrier
in those early years of the nineteenth century already
referred to.

.   By many around the countryside James Davidson of
Hindlee was supposed to be the " original " of Dandie Dinmont ; and not even Sir Walter Scott's asseverations to the contrary were sufficient to shake the popular faith in the oft-
expressed belief that the sturdy yeoman was in Scott's mind
when he gave to the world Dandie Dinmont.   At any rate,
this much we know—that Davidson had Terriers much of
the kind that Piper Allan had, that he differentiated only
by the names of Peppers and Mustards, names which even
to the present day are used by fanciers to describe the two
colours into which the Dandie Dinmont is divided.   Davidson died in 1820, and it is not until forty-one years after
(1861) that we are able to refer to this Terrier as an
acknowledged variety.   With a perversity that seems
characteristic of many of the older writers, detailed
descriptions of the dogs themselves are entirely lacking ;
while trustworthy illustrations portraying actual contemporary specimens are equally scarce.   In those days
there were not, it is true, the facilities for illustrations
that we enjoy now, yet one would have thought there must
exist somewhere paintings or engravings that with more or
less fidelity depicted the Terrier as it then was.   Most of
those we have seen have been more or less fanciful creations,
and their value as type-guides is not to be depended upon.
Sir Walter Scott was a great admirer of the Terrier, and
the life-like word-pictures that he presents of his own dogs
are always appreciated by lovers of these Terriers.   He
also had at Abbotsford at least one fine picture of the Dandie
Dinmont Terrier painted by Sir Edwin Landseer.

Early Patrons of the Breed.

At the time when the star of the Dandie Dinmont
Terrier began to be in the ascendant there was no lack

of noble patrons to espouse its cause. It mattered little to
the nobility of that period whether the dog looked a trifle
unkempt so long as its heart was in the right place when
the work it was required for had to be taken in hand.
Sir Walter Scott, we know, was an early admirer of the
Terrier for whose varietal name he was entirely responsible.
The Dukes of Northumberland, Buccleuch, and Roxburghe
also took up the breed, as did many of the principal county
magnates, in whom there existed an innate love of sport.
Still, though the variety had nobler patrons, yet it never
had a stauncher friend than the late Mr. E. Bradshaw
Smith, of Ecclefechan. To him present-day owners are
indebted not only for some of the best blood to be found,
but, what is of equal importance, for having for over forty
years kept a most methodically-compiled record of the pedigrees of those dogs found in his kennels; and it is entirely
due to this that the antecedents of many individuals may
be traced to those more remote times that we associate with
James Davidson. But to enumerate all who since the early
'seventies have worked in the breed's best interests would be
to fill many pages without any compensating advantages
being obtainable.

A Word-Picture of the Breed.

There is something unmistakably quaint about the
Dandie Dinmont Terrier that strikes even the most
unobservant; there is, too, something in the general build
and appearance that makes this Terrier stand out from
every other member of the great group. True, he shares
with his first-cousin the Bedlington Terrier the characteristic
topknot, but outwardly that is all one can point to in the
two Terriers in common. From every other variety of the
group he seems poles asunder both in conformation
and disposition. The late Mr. Thomson Gray, a thoroughly
capable breeder, judge, and versatile writer, truthfully
describes the Dandie as "the old man of the Terrier race—

wise, sensible, true in judgment, and tenacious to whatever
he takes a fancy, be it fur or feather. Stored up in that big,
sagacious domed head there is a lot of wisdom.   But for
the large, expressive eye, which at times lights up with fire,
one might regard the Dandie as a dull, sleepy dog that took
little or no notice of what was going on around him.   Let
anyone, however, tread on his tail or ask him to seek or
hunt rats, and you will see action! '' This graphic description fits the Terrier to the life, as everyone who has kept
it knows well.

Whether required for sport, as a house-dog, or purely
as a companion, this Terrier may be safely recommended.
Possessing an excellent temperament, and being slow to
anger, he differs materially from his near relative the
Bedlington.   It must not, however, be inferred from this
that he is not game; on the contrary, for his inches there is
no Terrier that is his superior.   We have seen the Dandie
used in various capacities, and to our mind he is one of
the best all round of the small dogs, irrespective of breed.
As a sporting Terrier his failing lies in his exceptionally hard
mouth.   Unlike the Scottish Terrier, he is not noisy, neither
is he headstrong, and therefore as a rabbit dog he should
find favour, except in the capacity of a retriever.   At the
very mention of the word '' Rats! '' he is at once ready for
the fray, and no better dog at such vermin can be found.
Intelligent, too, to a degree, it is quite an easy matter to
inculcate in this Terrier any lesson which a dog is capable
of learning.

Then, too, by reason of his colouring, the Terrier is one
that may be kept in the dirtiest of towns without the coat
showing signs of smoke and other discolorations as in
the case of a white or a light-coated breed.   Hardy the dog
undoubtedly is; what more, therefore, could be adduced in
praise of any dog?

Popularity at Shows.

For years this Terrier has been a popular show variety,
despite the fact that in the past it has been one of the breeds

coming under the ban of the " faker." Years ago it was quite a work of art to " prepare " this Terrier; and even now the breed is not free from the trimming taint. Still, it must, in justice to the Dandie Dinmont Terrier Club, be stated that since it was decided to keep the dog on more natural lines trimming has not been rife to anything like the same extent. The breeder has adopted natural rather than artificial means for the correction of defects of coat. As is the case with all dogs having drop ears, the Dandie as a puppy frequently needs a little ear manipulation between finger and thumb with a view to getting an otherwise refractory ear to assume the correct carriage. This, however, is legitimate preparation, and not to be compared with the ear-weighting that goes on even after the powers that be have pronounced it unfair. The topknot needs to be encouraged by good grooming and the use of an occasional stimulant. It must not be thought that this characteristic addition is in evidence from the first. On the contrary, it is months, not to say years, before a proper topknot can be cultivated. It is recorded of one of the most famous Dandies of modern times—Champion Tommy Atkins, whose portrait we give—that his topknot was not " sported " until he was well over three years old.

Peculiarities.

This is another of the Terriers showing a marked difference in coat in the puppy as compared with the adult. In the first place, the coat is quite short and soft, but gradually it takes on the correct texture. Peppers are born black, or black with tan legs and perhaps a white chest. Mustards are lighter (tan colour), but they have a good deal of black, especially down the back. Mr. Cook in his excellent works says :—" The ears, tail, and muzzle in mustard pups are often quite black, and if with this the crown shows a deep golden colour there is abundant promise." The two colours must be distinct; when they merge the one into the other the products are termed " saddlebacks." For

show purposes such dogs are, of course, useless. Too much
attention must not be paid to the eyes of puppies : these
often appear very light (blue-grey); eventually, however,
the dark eyes appear.

Noticeable Faults.

Much has been done by breeders to improve type. For
all that, there are some glaring faults to be seen in many
Dandies. Light eyes have already been alluded to; but there
is a tendency to perpetuate crooked-leg and large-eared
specimens, those having an arch of the body instead of in
the loin vicinity, soft coats, over-sized animals, skulls
that are flat rather than round or domed. The standard
laid down by the club is an ideal one; but there is no
reason why it should not be approached very closely if only
the breeder will eliminate the very undesirable elements that
are to be seen in many strains—really the outcome of
years of carelessness in respect of Dandie characteristics—
and enumerated above.

Clubs and Breed-Descriptions.

Followers of this breed are excellently catered for in
the matter of clubs, as they are in respect of a description
of their game little Terrier, the parent club being one of the
oldest of specialist clubs, having been founded in 1875. It
is also responsible for the following description—

Head.—Strongly made and large, not out of proportion to the
dog's size, the muscles showing extraordinary development, more
especially the maxillary. Skull broad between the ears, getting
gradually less towards the eyes, and measuring about the same
from the inner corner of the eye to back of skull as it does from ear
to ear. The forehead well domed. The head is *covered* with very
soft, silky hair, which should not be confined to a mere topknot,
and the lighter in colour and silkier it is the better. The cheeks,
starting from the ears proportionately with the skull, have a
gradual taper towards the muzzle, which is deep and strongly
made, and measures about 3in. in length, or in proportion to skull
as three is to five. The muzzle covered with hair of a little darker
shade than the topknot, and of the same texture as the feather of

the forelegs. The top of the muzzle is generally bare for about an inch from the back part of the nose, the bareness coming to a point towards the eye, and being about 1in. broad at the nose. The nose and inside of mouth black or dark-coloured. The teeth very strong, especially the canine, which are of extraordinary size for such a small dog. The canines fit well into each other, so as to give the greatest available holding and punishing power, and the teeth are level in front, the upper ones very slightly overlapping the under ones. [Many of the finest specimens have a "swine mouth," which is very objectionable, but is not so great an objection as the protrusion of the under jaw.]

Eyes.—Set wide apart, large, full, round, bright, expressive of great determination, intelligence, and dignity; set low and prominent in front of the head; colour, a rich dark hazel.

Ears.—Pendulous, set well back, wide apart, and low on the skull; hanging close to the cheeks, with a very slight projection at the base; broad at the junction of the head, and tapering almost to a point, the fore part of the ear tapering very little—the taper being mostly on the back part, the fore part of the ear coming almost straight down from its junction with the head to the tip. They should harmonise in colour with the body colour. In the case of a pepper dog they are covered with a soft, straight, brown hair (in some cases almost black). In the case of a mustard dog the hair should be mustard in colour, a shade darker than the body, but not black. All should have a thin feather of light hair starting about 2in. from the tip, and of nearly the same colour and texture as the topknot, which gives the ear the appearance of a *distinct point*. The animal is often one or two years old before the feather is shown. The cartilage and skin of the ear should not be thick, but rather thin. Length of ear, from 3in. to 4in.

Neck.—Very muscular, well developed, and strong, showing great power of resistance, being well set into the shoulders.

Body.—Long, strong, and flexible, ribs well sprung and round, chest well developed and let well down between the forelegs; the back rather low at the shoulder, having a slight downward curve and a corresponding arch over the loins, with a very slight gradual drop from top of loins to root of tail; both sides of backbone well supplied with muscle.

Tail.—Rather short, say from 8in. to 10in., and covered on the upper side with wiry hair of darker colour than that of the body, the hair on the under side being lighter in colour and not so wiry, with a nice feather about 2in. long, getting shorter as it nears the tip; rather thick at the root, getting thicker for about 4in., then tapering off to a point. It should not be twisted or curled in any way, but should come up with a regular curve like a scimitar, the tip, when excited, being in a perpendicular line with the root of the tail. It should neither be set on too high nor too low. When not excited it is carried gaily, and a little above the level of the body.

Legs.—The forelegs short, with immense muscular development and bone, set wide apart, the chest coming well down between them. The feet well formed, and not flat, with very strong brown or dark-coloured claws. Bandy legs and flat feet are objectionable. The hair on the fore legs and feet of a blue dog should be tan, varying according to the body colour, from a rich tan to a pale fawn; of a mustard dog they are of a darker shade than its head, which is a creamy white. In both colours there is a nice feather, about 2in. long, rather lighter in colour than the hair on the fore part of the leg. The hind-legs are a little longer than the fore ones, and are set rather wide apart, but not spread out in an unnatural manner, while the feet are much smaller; the thighs are well developed, and the hair of the same colour and texture as the forelegs, but having no feather or dewclaws; the whole claws should be dark, but the claws of all vary in shade according to the colour of the dog's body.

Coat.—This is a very important point; the hair should be about 2in. long, that from skull to root of tail a mixture of hardish and soft hair, which gives a sort of crisp feel to the hand. The hard should not be wiry; the coat is what is termed pily or pencilled. The hair on the under part of the body is lighter in colour and softer than on the top. The skin on the belly accords with the colour of the dog.

Colour.—The colour is pepper or mustard. The pepper colour ranges from a dark bluish black to a light silvery grey, the inter-mediate shades being preferred, the body colour coming well down the shoulder and hips, gradually merging into the leg colour. The mustards vary from a reddish-brown to a pale fawn, the head being a creamy white, the legs and feet of a shade darker than the head. The claws are dark, as in other colours. [Nearly all Dandie Din-mont Terriers have some white on the chest, and some have also white claws.]

Size.—The height should be from 8in. to 11in. at the top of shoulder. Length from top of shoulder to root of tail should not be more than twice the dog's height, but, preferably, 1in. or 2in. less.

Weight.—From 14lb. to 24lb., the best weight as near 18lb. as possible. These weights are for dogs in good working condition.

The relative values of the several points in the standard are apportioned as follow :—

	Value.
Head	10
Eyes	10
Ears	10
Neck	5
Body	20
Tail	5
Legs and Feet	10
Coat	15
Colour	5
Size and Weight	5
General appearance	5
Total	100

THE SCOTTISH TERRIER.

A Confused Breed.

No breed of Terrier in the past has been more confused than this. By writers at different times he has been dubbed a Skye Terrier, and, indeed, illustrated as such; while the multiplicity of popular names by which he is known has tended to add to the confusion. Diehard, Cairn, Broken-haired Terrier, and Aberdeen Terrier are a quartet of names bestowed upon it, and appropriately bestowed except in the case of the last, which is, in our opinion, a misnomer and will be dealt with elsewhere. The first is obviously in allusion to its game qualities, and is as appropriate as it is just; for Scottie is undoubtedly ever ready to assume the defensive. The second has reference to the calling of the working dog, which is to oust from the " cairns " (the conical heaps of stones) the foxes which take shelter there. This primitive method of fox-hunting is very different from what obtains in England. As a matter of fact it is a necessary measure of protection on the part of the Highland sheep-farmers, and is undertaken by a foxhunter—as primitive almost as the dwelling in which he ofttimes resides—a brace of sturdy Terriers, and perhaps a hound. He carries a firearm, and with it makes short work of Reynard when bolted. The term " Broken-haired Terrier " is too obvious to need any explanation.

There are some enthusiasts—quite a number in fact—who regard the Scottish Terrier as a very ancient breed; there are others who, while recognising a Scottish Terrier, consider it but a comparatively modern product. Among the latter are Colonel Malcolm of Poltalloch, whose strain of West Highland White Terriers we have dealt with elsewhere. The late Mr. Thomson Gray, no mean authority on all that pertained to the dogs of Scotland, the late Mr. Rawdon Lee, and many others, on the contrary, believe the variety to have existed from time immemorial in the islands and Highlands of Scotland. Be that as it may, it has little bearing upon the popularity of the dog, which seems now as firmly established in the southern half as it has been for many years prior in the northern half of Great Britain. Rather more than thirty years ago the perky little Terrier which has now found so many admirers in the South was practically unknown. It was left to the late Captain Mackie so to improve the breed that it obtained a hold here; while he was ably backed up in his endeavours by Mr. H. J. Ludlow, and Messrs. Adamson, Spelman, Hammond, Blomfield, &c. The variety did not make any real progress as a show dog until the " eighties " of the last century, when its good qualities and " the money " they brought introduced it prominently to the notice of the dog-loving public generally, and the breed has never seriously looked back. A specialist club followed as a natural consequence the rise into favour of the breed—this was in 1882—and it is a very short time after that we find not only a readable but a practical description of the variety drawn up.

The Prefix "Aberdeen."

So commonly is this name employed as if it were a varietal one that it is necessary to say something under this head. First, there is no Terrier that may be rightly so regarded; and it is difficult, if not well-nigh impossible, to state how the name originated. Practically every specimen dubbed an Aberdeen Terrier that we have seen has been a coarse sort of make-believe Scottish Terrier, and as far removed in type from the real article as the modern representative of the show-ring, with its extra long head, is from the original Scotch or Fox Terrier, as it was and is frequently called.

A Disturbing Factor.

Were we asked to name the most disturbing factor in connection with the history of the breed, we should unhesitatingly point to the great trimming question. It was this that proved the stumbling-block to even still greater progress, for those people who loved the dog to appear in the garb that Nature intended could not tolerate the coat-stripping that

A Typical Scotch Terrier—Mrs. Hannay's Champion Villain.

the fanciers of the time indulged in—a practice, be it said, that obtains to the present day, though to nothing like the same extent. In 1900 Mr. Ludlow, the most successful breeder of the Terrier since it was dignified by the name of a variety, wrote very strongly against the amount of trimming that was indulged in by fanciers of the breed, and did not mince matters as to what was likely to happen were it continued. Wiser counsels have prevailed since his note of warning was sounded, and though Scottie is not " barbered " to the extent it once was, it nevertheless requires a fairly skilful " trimmer " to put the dog down in the show-ring with the coat that Fashion (in contradistinction to Nature) has decreed shall obtain. Practically all the long coat was pulled out by the trimmer of old, but the modern man seems to have hit upon some labour-saving appliances that do the work that once devolved on finger and thumb combined with the trimming-comb. The whole business of trimming is unsavoury, and would not be alluded to at all were it not necessary to put the novice attracted by this Terrier on his guard. For instance, he might readily purchase from the show-bench a winning specimen that, after three months' ordinary treatment in the matter of grooming, might have a coat that for length would seem to belong to another animal.

Qualities and Temperament.

Every breed of Terrier seems to possess some individual characteristic that is not recognised until after it has been carefully studied by an owner for some considerable time. To see Scottie on the show-bench, or while on the *qui vive* for something that is for the moment engaging his attention, or as he trots complacently after his master or mistress in a crowded thoroughfare, one would certainly not suspect him of being "stand-offish" as regards everyone except them. Yet that trait is unmistakably marked directly one has the opportunity for studying the dog at home. Though he will obey certain commands given by others, yet he seems to recognise but one master or mistress, and for either he would sacrifice his life. He is a most affectionate little fellow, smart, as hard as nails, and a capital vermin-dog. Intelligent, too, he certainly is, and for a companion or house-dog we should want nothing better. A trifle headstrong, a wee bit noisy on "fur," and, when not checked, not over-particular as regards his quarry, he is nevertheless very amenable to discipline. Like the rest of the Terriers he is hard in mouth, and not a little patience has to be bestowed on his education if he is to prove of any use as an assistant to the

gunner who does not keep a sporting field-dog proper. We
should not regard Scottie as a quarrelsome dog; nor, on the
other hand, should we class him a "soft." He is an even-
tempered chap; but woe betide any dog about his size and
weight, or a little over, that wounds his pride, for he will
be certain to have "one off." No Terrier his size that we
can call to mind has such big teeth or can bite so hard as
Scottie, and the punishment he is capable of inflicting is
altogether out of proportion to his size. Despite his short
legs and somewhat peculiar conformation, he is very active,
and will, moreover, go through a long and tiring day without
showing any sign of fatigue. We have worked one of these
dogs in rough heather and furze country all day, and he never
seemed sick or sorry. Scottie is equally good in the water.
We have kept and bred many of these Terriers, and, so far
as our experience went, they seemed very prone to a stubborn
form of eczema—a sort of inherent tendency. Save for
that, we have nothing but praise for the breed as a whole,
whether regarded purely as a companion or in the dual
capacity of watcher and worker. For the latter purpose,
however, they need to be small. Some of the large, coarse,
over-sized animals that are often dignified by the name of
"Aberdeens," and passed on to the unsuspecting as the real
article, would be of not the slightest use for such purpose.

Housing the Dog.

Some may wonder why, in face of the fact that there is a
chapter devoted to housing, it is necessary to say anything
here under the head. The fact is, the Scottish Terrier is
one of those breeds that are best kept outside, in a thoroughly
rain- and draught-proof kennel. Thus treated he is not so
likely to develop a long, shaggy coat as he is when kept
entirely in the house. Our own plan was to kennel Scottie
outside all day, and at night to bring him in to guard the premises. Moreover, the indoor-grown coat is, generally speaking, softer and woollier than that produced on the dog when
kennelled outside. Again, so far as our own experience

is concerned Scottie seems to prefer an outside kennel (of course, not chained), where he can note what is going on, to being kept indoors. Still, it must not be deduced therefrom that he is incapable of appreciating a seat in front of the fire; for, on the contrary, he likes it, and appreciates it the more when he is allowed to have such a position by way of a treat.

A Notable Colour-sport.

For some years now the frequenters of the larger provincial gatherings have been made acquainted with a white (or whitish) Scottish Terrier. Though as regards type it does not, on the whole, so closely approximate to the usual colour met with, yet it is sufficiently near thereto to be readily recognised. When the dog first came out there were many novices who fondly imagined that this was the Roseneath, West Highland White, or Poltalloch Terrier. Nothing, however, could be more erroneous. It is quite a modern colour-sport of the dog that for many years now we have been accustomed to admire as a Scottish Terrier, and altogether different in type from the latter variety, which has been dealt with elsewhere in this manual. How it originated is, perhaps, not known with certainty; but we have a very vivid recollection of the late Captain Keene (the old Fox-Terrier breeder) possessing one of these white (or whitish) Scottish Terriers. Still the chief breeder has been Dr. Flaxman, of Pittenweem, and some very good specimens have seen the light. These whitish Scottish Terriers are, as already stated, different from the West Highland White Terrier, which is more closely related to the fox-hunting type of Skye Terrier. Anyone interested in the two breeds will see a marked difference if specimens of the respective varieties are placed side by side. By comparison, the muzzle of the West Highland Terrier is far lighter, and the head generally is quite different. Although this " sport " is supposed to be white, yet many specimens met with are creamy rather than white; while, instead of having black noses,

they are often flesh-coloured.   Some enthusiastic followers
of this strain of Scottish Terrier go so far as to assert that
the breed was originally white.   There is, however, nothing
to warrant the assumption, so far as we know.   There can be
little doubt that a white or a light-coloured dog is far better
for sporting purposes than the darker, or even the sandy-
coloured one, as it is not so liable to be taken at a
distance for the quarry.   Breeders, however, have much leeway to make up before this white " sport " can truly be
reckoned the equal or type of its darker relatives.

The Long-head Craze.

There is, and has been for some time, a danger of
breeders sacrificing really typical qualities for an exaggerated
length of head, though for what purpose we have never been
able to divine.   The late Mr. Thomson Gray, who knew
Scottish Terriers about as well as anyone, directed attention
to this twenty years ago; and there have been many breeders
since who have condemned the exaggeration; still it
continues.   The head should be in correct proportion to the
other body-measurements, and not out of relation thereto,
as is frequently the case.   With the very long heads, square
muzzles, full light eyes, much of the expression is lost; while
the extra long head, when shown on a comparatively short
body, makes the dog look untypical.   As well as a craze for
a long head, there seems to have arisen a desire for longer
legs, and here again the modern Scottish Terrier loses a good
deal of that character associated with the working type of
dog, which should, after all, be the model if the word
Terrier is to be correctly associated therewith.   Scottie was
originally a low, heavily-built dog, and was employed, as
we have stated elsewhere, for a specific purpose.   Since
his " improvers " have had him in hand they have, in
several directions, allowed their zeal to outrun their discretion; hence the exaggerated types that are seen at practically
every show.   Coats, too, lack that pin-wire, pig-bristle feel
that the older specimens of the breed had.   The fact is, the

hard outer coat, if it should happen to be longer than desirable, is pulled out in show specimens some time in advance of the date for which the dog is required, and when the hand is run through the jacket of such a dog it is the soft, dense undercoat that is felt.   Little wonder, therefore, that the "ideal" descriptions of the breed furnished appear to the novice to be at such variance with the accepted ideas of judges as reflected at shows.   We say to the novice advisedly, for the old hand at exhibiting is, of course, perfectly well aware of the amount of trimming that goes on. Indeed, unless a fancier of the Scottish Terrier is prepared to trim, he will stand very little chance in open competitions.

Clubs and Description.

The Scottish Terrier is not lacking in that support specialists can furnish, for it has two most powerful bodies in the Scottish Terrier Club of England and the Scottish Terrier Club of Scotland, to say nothing of others.   As regards a description of the breed, we give that drawn up by the latter body :—

Skull.—Proportionately long, slightly domed, and covered with short, hard hair, about ¾in. long, or less.   It should not be quite flat, as there should be a sort of stop, or drop, between the eyes.

Muzzle.—Very powerful, and gradually tapering towards the nose, which should always be black and of a good size.   The jaw should be perfectly level, and the teeth square, though the nose projects somewhat over the mouth, which gives the impression of the upper jaw being longer than the lower one.

Eyes.—A dark brown or hazel colour; small, piercing, very bright, and rather sunken.

Ears.—Very small, prick or half-prick (the former is preferable), but never drop.   They should also be sharp-pointed, and the hair on them should not be long, but velvety, and they should not be cut.   The ears should be free from any fringe at the top.

Neck.—Short, thick, and muscular; strongly set on sloping shoulders.

Chest.—Broad in comparison to the size of the dog, and proportionately deep.

Body.—Of moderate length, but not so long as a Skye's, and rather flat-sided; well ribbed up, and exceedingly strong in hindquarters.

Legs and Feet.—Both fore and hind legs should be short, and very heavy in bone, the former being straight, and well set on under the body, as the Scotch Terrier should not be "out at elbows." The hocks should be bent, and the thighs very muscular; and the feet strong, small, and thickly covered with short hair, the fore feet being larger than the hind ones.

The Tail, which is never cut, should be about 7in. long, carried with a slight bend, and often gaily.

The Coat should be rather short (about 2in.), intensely hard and wiry in texture, and very dense all over the body.

Size.—From 15lb. to 20lb.; the best weight being as near as possible about 18lb. for dogs and 16lb. for bitches, when in condition for work.

Colours.—Steel or iron grey, black-brindle, grey-brindle, black, sandy, and wheaten. White markings are objectionable, and can only be allowed on the chest and to a small extent.

General Appearance.—The face should wear a very sharp, bright, and active expression, and the head should be carried up. The dog (owing to the shortness of his coat) should appear to be higher on the leg than he really is; but, at the same time, he should look compact, and possessed of great muscle in his hindquarters. In fact, a Scotch Terrier, though essentially a Terrier, cannot be too powerfully put together, and should be from 9in. to 12in. in height.

SPECIAL FAULTS.

Muzzle.—Either under- or over-hung.

Eyes.—Large or light-coloured.

Ears.—Large, round at the points, or drop. It is also a fault if they are too heavily covered with hair.

Legs.—Bent, or slightly bent at elbows.

Coat.—Any silkiness, wave, or tendency to curl is a serious blemish, as is also an open coat.

Size.—Specimens over 20lb. should not be encouraged.

SCALE OF POINTS.

Skull	$7\frac{1}{2}$
Muzzle	$7\frac{1}{2}$
Eyes	5
Ears	5
Neck	5
Chest	5
Body	15
Legs and Feet	10
Tail	$2\frac{1}{2}$
Coat	15
Size	10
Colour	$2\frac{1}{2}$
General Appearance	10
Total	100

THE SKYE TERRIER.

A Much Discussed Variety.

So far as we can call to mind, no individual breed of Terrier has been so hotly discussed as the subject of this chapter. We quite well remember what may be called *the* great discussion that was continued for so many weeks in the columns of the *Country*, and we are fairly well acquainted with the other important contributions upon the subject that have appeared since. None of them, however, have led to finality as regards the much-vexed question as to what the early progenitors of the present-day Skye Terrier were like, and we are very much in the same position to-day in respect thereof as were the fanciers of the seventies. It is, we know, high treason even to suggest in the presence of many enthusiasts that the Skye Terrier is a modern production. Yet if the question is viewed in that impartial spirit that should obtain, and moreover in a practical light, the only reasonable conclusion that can be arrived at is that the present-day long-coated dog is not identical with the working Terrier that we read about as being found on the Western Islands of Scotland and used by the crofters for hunting the foxes from the cairns (heaps of stones), and a very few moments' reflection should suffice to convince even the most enthusiastic present-day Skye Terrier lover of the absurdity of the claims put forth for it by some in regard to its working qualities.

It is only natural, of course, that every ardent admirer of a breed should wish to trace its origin as far back as possible. With quite a large number of Skye Terrier enthusiasts there is a desire to show that the present-day dog is a direct descendant of that

Terrier to which the interesting sixteenth-century writer, Dr. Caius, refers in his " Englishe Dogges." The probability is that the Terrier of that time was more closely allied to the variety that is fast coming into prominence—the West Highland White Terrier, which we know to have been kept purely as a worker for at least a century. This seems a far more reasonable assumption than that the long-haired dog we now designate a Skye Terrier is one and the same Terrier as that referred to by Caius.

Everyone who has taken up the breeding of dogs in a practical fashion must know how easy it is to produce under more or less artificial conditions certain coat characteristics. For proof of this we need look no further than to the Yorkshire Terrier, whose abnormal length of coat is generally admitted to be largely due to the conditions under which the dog is kept. Our own view of the matter is that the present-day Skye Terrier, with its long jacket, is a comparatively modern production—an outcome, as it were, of the era of dog shows.

The late Mr. Thomson Gray and Mr. Rawdon Lee— the former probably the greatest authority on the dogs of Scotland, and the latter scarcely, if any, less renowned in regard to those of England—both unhesitatingly state that the Skye Terrier as we know it is a modern creation—a view that, for the reasons we have already adduced, we quite endorse. For all that, this distinctive Terrier has now bred true to type for a number of years, and we must therefore leave its early origin in much the same obscurity as that surrounding many another prominent breed identified with Scotland.

Legends concerning the way the original Skye Terrier was or was not evolved have been rife, but none of them that have come down to us will bear the light of day turned on to them. The " prettiest," and we may say the most unlikely, is that the dog owes its origin to mere chance, and goes back to the days of the Spanish Armada. Some of the vessels of that ill-fated fleet were supposed to have gone ashore on the Western coasts, and with them some " Spanish white dogs," that eventually interbred with the native dogs of the Western Isles!

It is interesting and instructive to go through such records as the Kennel Club Stud Book furnishes, and also to note the number of entries that the exhibitions of the time attracted. From these the status of the breed at different decades may be deduced with fair accuracy. Just now the dog has an excellent following, and signs are not wanting that make for further progress. These we shall deal with in their proper sequence.

Ever since we have had any reliable records of dogs and dog shows, the Skye Terrier, if not a fashionable dog in the much-abused sense of that term, has had at least a fair following. Further, there have been breeders who paid very close attention to certain strains of which they were the possessors—the Dukes of Argyll, the Malcolms of Poltalloch, the Camerons, &c. Indeed, it was from the first-named nobleman that the late Queen Victoria received one of the famous working dogs that at the time were kept for the purpose of ousting the foxes from their underground retreats. These strains live in the West Highland White Terrier of to-day.

Prick- and Drop-eared—Creams and Fawns.

Two varieties of the Skye Terrier are met with, differing only in the matter of ear-carriage—the prick- and the drop-eared. The latter is the older type of ear, though just at present the former is the more favoured. Still, the admirers of the drop-eared type are increasing rapidly. It has been asserted that the prick-ear was obtained through a cross with the Scottish Terrier. Whether this is so or not matters very little now, as the dog breeds true to type, though it is not at all infrequent for drop-eared puppies to be produced in the litters of prick-eared parents, thus showing the influence exerted by their remote ancestors. In all other points, save that of actual ear-carriage, the two types are practically identical. We say " practically " because there is just a slight difference in ear-placement in the two forms, the drop-ears being set on the head somewhat lower than the prick-ears.

Hear, too, we might very well refer to the colour-varieties known as creams and golden fawns that are all too seldom met with nowadays of anything like the correct type. They

Mrs. Wilmer's Skye Terrier Champion Yexford Longfellow.

are very desirable and attractive, and deserve to have greater attention paid to them.

Sporting Qualities, Temperament, Constitution, &c.

Classified, as it is, as a sporting breed, one naturally looks for something to justify its inclusion in such a category, but in vain. Sporting instincts the dog undoubtedly

has, and capabilities for using them. Picture the result to
an 8in. or 9in. coated modern Skye engaged in its native
country on the work for which it was by nature intended
before dog shows claimed it! It would present a sorry sight,
and be quite incapable of performing its allotted task of
bolting Reynard from his fastnesses—the mission the dog was
called upon to perform half a century or so ago and earlier.
Enthusiastic as we are over the many good qualities which
endear this variety to the lover of dogs generally, we

Mrs. Wilmer's Drop-Eared Skye Terrier Champion Young Ivanhoe of Yoxford.

nevertheless maintain that it should properly be classed
as an ornamental variety. That the Skye Terrier makes
a most companionable, smart dog, even its worst enemies
will admit, but fanciers, in their desire for extra long coats,
have quite spoilt the dog for the serious outdoor work of
the hardy Terriers.

That the opinion we have expressed is not universally
shared by the many admirers of the breed is shown by the
following extract from a letter we have received from
Mrs. Wilmer dealing with the point, and after she had
seen our remarks thereon. She writes :—" Forgive me if I
venture to differ from the writer when he underrates the

sporting proclivities and capabilities of Skyes. The heavy
coats do not impede them one bit when hunting; neither
does mud or wet injure the coat, provided the dog be allowed
to dry naturally in a kennel with a bed of absorbent sawdust.
Champion Yoxford Ivanhoe has been shot over repeatedly,
and he was a splendid ratter, in spite of a long, heavy coat
of a golden fawn hue. My old Yoxford Blue Boy (a winner
in his day) at eight years old is constantly used for keeping
down rats on a farm near by; and a young bitch of my own
breeding recently killed twenty rats in one afternoon at her
first attempt. I had to put my old cat to sleep, as my long-
coats nearly finished him off, though he would turn any stray
dog out of the garden. An acquaintance of mine often uses
his Skyes when out shooting, as they are excellent retrievers."

Judging from our experience of the breed, we should be
inclined to class the variety as one that was devotedly
attached to the master, mistress, or other person with whom
it was constantly brought in contact, but "stand-offish" in
respect of all others, thus resembling the Scottish Terrier
and one or two others. Intelligent, smart as a house-dog, and
not wanting in gameness are other qualities that may be
ascribed to the breed as a whole; and these even its worst
detractors will allow.

Probably by the majority of casual observers of the
variety it would be written down as a delicate breed, but
this is far from being the case, as it is one of those Terriers
that, if properly reared and housed, may be allowed to
lead an outdoor life the year round. To coddle such a dog
by providing it with artificially-heated kennels is a great mistake, and the sooner the prospective Skye Terrier fancier
recognises it the better for the variety. We have seen
excellent litters of Skye Terriers reared outside in winter,
though, if it can be avoided, it is always inadvisable to do so.
There is nothing like spring and summer for rearing puppies
healthily, and practical fanciers select those seasons simply
because of the amount of bright sunshine that is reasonably
to be expected. Sunshine and fresh air are two very valu-

able aids to puppy-rearing, and without them the tenderest
of care and the most rational of food will not avail.

Kennel Management.

We have already suggested that as regards kennels
nothing special is called for.   All that is wanted is a well-
constructed, airy, light, damp-proof structure placed in
such a position that sunshine reaches the kennel and its
occupants.   When, however, we come to consider what has
to be done if we would " put down " this dog in first-class
show condition, we must confess that some difficulties in
regard to coat preparation present themselves.   As to feeding,
this does not differ from that obtaining in the case of any
other hardy Terrier, though in all cases where extra length
of jacket is required a little fat given to the individual dog is
beneficial rather than harmful.   In feeding, the greatest care
needs to be exercised to prevent any irritation of the skin, for
this would be fatal to the dog's chances of obtaining a prize.
A well-balanced dietary of meat, bread, and biscuit should,
therefore, be provided.   It is a mistake to think that meat
is not good for these long-coated dogs.   A fair proportion
of cooked lean meat, as a rule, should be given with a base of
stale bread, or biscuit free from meat.   Now and again a little
finely-shredded raw meat may with advantage be fed to
most dogs.   Cod-liver oil biscuits in change will be of advantage in the production of coat.

This Terrier is one of the few that may be kept in fairly
good condition on a minimum of exercise ; but it must not
be deduced from this that exercise may only be given by
fits and starts : it should be regular, and to a certain extent
the owner must be guided by weather conditions, as a
tremendous lot of work would be entailed, to say nothing
of the chances of injury to the coat, if the dog were exercised
in bad weather.   A good run to the kennels should therefore
be provided : it should be laid with one or other of the
substances referred to in the chapter dealing with kennel

construction, should have an aspect in which it would be readily dried by sun and air, and should be covered over. Even this limited space would help to keep the dogs healthy in bad weather; while if a grass enclosure of some sort could be allowed them to scamper over when the weather was favourable, this would be very beneficial. All that would be necessary in addition would be a little road exercise, which is good for every dog—long- or short-coated.

Preparation for Show.

We now come to a most important part of our subject, and one, as is the case with Terriers generally, that is beset with difficulties. Here we are face to face with the problem of—to grease or not to grease. There are advocates of both systems, each section of which states that good results are to be obtained. Mrs. Wilmer was, we think, the first prominent fancier openly to declare against the " greasing " of these long-coated dogs, and as she practises what she preaches, and has attained a very high position in the Kennel World on account of her Skye Terriers, her very practical suggestions are entitled to the greatest respect. Moreover, as she has practically demonstrated the fact that it is possible to grow on a Skye Terrier the coat beloved of the fancy without the trouble and mess inseparable from the " greasy " method, the advantages of the one over the other are apparent.

In dealing with the Yorkshire Terrier in the first volume, the " grease " method of coat-growing was fully explained. There is, therefore, no need to repeat the details here. Naturally there will be advocates of both methods, and the disciples of each will follow which they think the better. Though the Skye Terrier in respect of length of jacket may be compared with the Yorkshire Terrier, yet in texture it differs materially, being far harder—quite wiry in fact. Many Skye Terriers when prepared on the old system of greasing and washing them are so combed and brushed

D

that the protective under-coat is very little in evidence. That
it is necessary to remove all dead coat goes without saying.
Unless the old coat be removed the new and fast coat
cannot get through, and the dog suffers considerably in
appearance as a consequence.

Mrs. Wilmer in her very instructive monograph on
the Skye most emphatically states that these Terriers
prepared on the old method of keeping them more or less
in grease, constantly washing and grooming them, "present
a chipped appearance" from the processes to which they
have been subjected, to say nothing of the fact that their coats
are appreciably darkened and to that extent suffer. Our own
experience is that scarcely two dogs of any breed of Terrier
require exactly identical preparation, each individual being a
law unto itself in that respect. That many long-coated dogs
required for show suffer from too much grooming may be
admitted, and the owner should therefore use considerable
discretion about the combing and brushing.

Mrs. Wilmer further states that many Skye Terriers will
go for weeks without anything being applied to the coat at
all, not even a brush. We must confess that we have
never tried the effect of such treatment on a Skye Terrier,
but we see not the slightest reason to doubt the practicability
of Mrs. Wilmer's practice; on the contrary, we see a good
deal of reason and common sense in it. That it must be a
great saving of trouble is certain, and when once the general
public realises the fact that the lengthy and tedious
processes formerly associated with the preparation of the
show Skye Terrier are no longer necessary or indeed
desirable, one of the greatest bars to the breed's progress
will have been removed. The stimulant that Mrs. Wilmer
advocates is paraffin and neat's-foot oil (one part of the
former to three of the latter); and as this is a preparation
that we have ourselves advocated for twenty years, nothing
further need be said here on the point.

If a well-groomed Skye Terrier be examined just before
it is "put down" ready for the judge, it will be seen that

there is a parting extending from the face to the tail.
To obtain the level parting will require a good deal of
practice, and it will be a good plan for the novice to see
how an experienced fancier performs the operation.   No
amount of book-reading will atone for lack of practice. What
may be termed the face fringe requires delicate manipulation
if the dog is to look its best.   The two illustrations that
we give will suggest how the coat should be disposed.   As
we stated in Yorkshire Terriers, special brushes and combs
are required for that and similar varieties.

Bedding.

Long-coated varieties of dogs require something quite
different for a bed from what would suffice for their short-
coated relatives.   In winter a Petanelle rug instead of
straw (which must not be employed) would suffice ; while
in summer this might be dispensed with altogether.   Or again,
improvised cushions (enclosing paper shavings) as advocated
for the Yorkshire Terrier might be tried.   Nothing likely
to harbour fleas should be used, as such external parasites
would cause the dog to scratch and break its coat.   Every
precaution, therefore, against their establishing themselves in
a kennel must be taken.

Present-day Faults.

Although excellent standards to which the Skye Terrier
should be bred are in existence, there is a tendency on the
part of some fanciers to depart from the type therein laid
down.   One of the chief faults of the Skye Terrier is that
it is often found too big.   It is this striving after extra size
and extra length of coat that has tended to the production
of specimens with anything but level backs, light eyes, badly-
carried tails, and soft coats.   Roach-backed Skye Terriers are
far from uncommon, and they are certainly undesirable where
show dogs are concerned.   Still many breeders noticed the
deterioration in type that was taking place, and have altered

their tactics; so that in the future we may see Skyes of the
type that we associate with the days when Mr. James Pratt
was such a power in the fancy.

Colour in Young Puppies.

As is the case with the Yorkshire Terrier, the Skye
Terrier as a puppy is very different in colour from the adult.
At birth and for some time after the puppies are black, or
with perhaps a greyish face. Gradually they assume the
correct colours, and the coat begins to lengthen, though it is
not until they are well advanced that the long jacket is in
evidence.

Clubs, and Description of the Breed.

Three specialist clubs look after this variety—the Skye
Terrier and Clydesdale Terrier Club, the Skye Terrier Club
of England, and the Skye Terrier Club of Scotland. Each
of these bodies has drawn up an excellent description of the
breed that should commend itself to the practical fancier.
The following emanates from the last-named body :—

Head.—Long, with powerful jaws and incisor teeth closing
level, or upper just fitting over lower. Skull wide at front of
brow, narrowing between ears, and tapering gradually towards
muzzle, with little falling in between or behind the eyes. Eyes
hazel, medium size, close set. Muzzle always black.

Ears (prick or pendent).—When *prick*, not large, erect at outer
edges, and slanting towards each other at inner, from peak to skull.
When *pendent,* larger, hanging straight, lying flat, and close at
front.

Body.—Pre-eminently long and low. Shoulders broad, chest
deep, ribs well sprung and oval-shaped, giving flattish appearance
to sides. Hindquarters and flank full and well developed. Back
level and slightly declining from top of hip joint to shoulders.
Neck long and gently crested.

Tail.—When *hanging,* upper half perpendicular, under half
thrown backwards in a curve. When *raised,* a prolongation of the
incline of the back, and not rising higher nor curling up.

Legs.—Short, straight, and muscular. No dew claws. Feet large and pointing forward.

Coat (double).—An *under,* short, close, soft, and woolly. An *over,* long—averaging 5½in.—hard, straight, flat, and free from crisp or curl. Hair on head shorter, softer, and veiling forehead and eyes; on ears, overhanging inside, falling down and mingling with side locks, not heavily, but surrounding the ear like a fringe, and allowing its shape to appear. Tail also gracefully feathered.

Colour (any variety).—Dark or light blue or grey, or fawn with black points. Shade of head and legs approximating that of body.

STANDARD.

1.—AVERAGE MEASURE.

Dog.—Height, at shoulder, 9in.
 Length, back of skull to root of tail, 22½in.
 ,, muzzle to back of skull, 8½in.
 ,, root of tail to top joint, 9in.
 Total length, 40in.

Bitch.—Half an inch lower, and 2½in. shorter than dog, all parts proportional; thus, body 21in., head 8in., and tail 8½in.; total, 37½in.

2.—AVERAGE WEIGHT.

Dog, 18lb.; bitch, 16lb.
No dog should be over 20lb. nor under 16lb.; and no bitch should be over 18lb. nor under 14lb.

3.—POINTS, WITH VALUE. Max.

1. *Size.*	Height with	10 inches high	.	.	5	15
	Length and	9 ,, ,,	.	.	10	
	Proportions,	8½ ,, ,,	.	.	15	
	Scale for bitches ½in. lower throughout.					
2. *Head.*	Skull and Eyes	.	.	.	10	15
	Jaws and Teeth	.	.	.	5	
3. *Ears.*	Carriage, with Shape, Size and Feather					10
4. *Body.*	Back and Neck	.	.	.	10	15
	Chest and Ribs	.	.	.	5	
5. *Tail.*	Carriage and Feather	.	.	.		10
6. *Legs.*	Straightness and Shortness	.	.	5	10
	Strength	.	.	.	5	

7. *Coat.*	Hardness	.	.	.	.	.	.	10	}
	Lankness	.	.	.	.	.	.	5	} 20
	Length	.	.	.	.	.	.	5	}
8. *Colour and Condition*		.	.	.	.	.	.	5	

Total   100

4.—JUDICIAL AWARDS.

1. Over extreme weight to be handicapped 5 per lb. of excess.
2. Over- or under-shot mouths to disqualify.
3. Doctored ears or tail to disqualify.
4. No extra value for greater length of coat than 5½in.
5. Not to be commended under a total of 60. Not to be highly commended under a total of 65. Not to be very highly commended under a total of 70. No specials to be given under a total of 75.

THE WEST HIGHLAND WHITE TERRIER.

Antiquity of the Breed.

To many, perhaps to the majority, of Terrier-lovers this very distinctive Scottish variety is unknown even by name. Yet it is no new breed, having been in existence probably for centuries; while it has been kept for at least a century in all its purity by the Malcolms of Poltalloch, in Argyll-shire. Indeed, from this latter fact the dog, when first it came South, was frequently dubbed the Poltalloch Terrier. Those who study the early history of our Terriers, or at least that portion of it that may be regarded as authentic, must carefully bear this in mind, as there are not a few who confuse with this distinctive dog the White Scottish Terrier that of late years has been produced. If, however, one will carefully scan two representative specimens of these breeds it will at once be seen that they are widely different, a point that the Kennel Club has not been slow to recognise, having bestowed on the West Highland White Terrier last year the hall-mark of varietal rank. The White Scottish Terrier has barely a quarter of a century's record, whereas the other Terrier, as we have already stated, is a centenarian at least.

There seems to be very little doubt that the Roseneath Terrier (classes for which were a few years ago provided at Cruft's) was practically identical with the dog that to-day is known by the name here adopted. We, of course, refer to the Simon Pure article, for there seems to be at least more than an element of doubt that Clark, one of the Duke of Argyll's keepers on the Roseneath estates, had not that fine regard for purity of blood as we are warranted in supposing exists in the Poltalloch strain.   Hence, therefore, the difference in type exhibited by the two strains.

A Workman Purely and Simply.

Lest in these strenuous days, when even dog shows suffer from the pace at which we go, there may be any doubt in the minds of Terrier-lovers as to the kind of dog the West Highland White Terrier is, we may say that it is a

A typical West Highland White Terrier—one of Colonel Malcolm's.

workman in every sense of the word, kept in the land of its birth for ousting the fox, the badger, and the otter from their rocky fastnesses.   To face foes like these under such conditions calls for considerable activity and plenty of courage; and both of these are to be found in the real article.   It will, therefore, be a thousand pities if, in the attempts to make this a popular Terrier, it is allowed to deteriorate as a workman.   We well know the fate that has overtaken the Skye Terrier, and, to a lesser extent

perhaps, the Scottish and the Dandie Dinmont Terriers.
All these originally were working dogs; but to-day, even
were they fitted in other respects, they are far too valuable
as show animals to be employed as workmen. Eventually,
therefore, such qualities as once distinguished them will
die out simply from never being called into play.
So far as Colonel Malcolm's strain is concerned the dogs
are always schooled in their legitimate business; and
though there are undoubtedly many other game Terriers
that could " face the music " at any of the vermin named,
yet the conditions under which they would be found in
England would be vastly different from those obtaining in
the wild West Highlands.

Compared with the White Scottish Terrier.

Though there are certain points of resemblance between
the Scottish Terrier proper and the West Highland White
Terrier, yet there are also many points of differentiation. One
of the first to strike the student of breeds is the much lighter
muzzle of the West Highland White Terrier, the fuller,
softer coat (more particularly in the neck vicinity, where
it forms quite a ruff), and the more " business-like "
appearance generally. There is already a tendency on the
part of the present-day fanciers to improve on Nature by
giving these dogs prick-ears, whereas, as Colonel Malcolm
points out, a drop or a half-drop ear would be more useful
in the case of the working dog, though he does not attempt
to deny the smartness imparted by ears of the other kind.
Up to the present this dog, unlike its relative the Scottish
Terrier, has been allowed to carry a natural coat; but
probably, as time goes on, trimming will be introduced into
the preparation of this breed, and with disastrous results,
if the dog is to be recognised as a working and not merely
as an ornamental variety. The club which has been formed
to watch over the breed should not forget this, and should
endeavour, at all risks, to maintain the well-deserved
reputation of this plucky little Scotch Terrier. There is

a good demand for the variety, and at prices that should make it remunerative to the breeder.

Description.

Hereunder is given a description of the breed as drawn up by the West Highland White Terrier Club :—

The General Appearance of the West Highland White Terrier is that of a small, game, hardy-looking Terrier, possessed with no small amount of self-esteem, with a varminty appearance, strongly built, deep in chest and back ribs, straight back and powerful quarters on muscular legs, and exhibiting in a marked degree a great combination of strength and activity. The coat should be about 2½in. long, white in colour, hard, with plenty of soft undercoat, and no tendency to wave or curl. The tail should be as straight as possible and carried not too gaily, and covered with hard hair, but not bushy. The skull should not be too broad, being in proportion to the terribly powerful jaws. The ears should be as small and sharp-pointed as possible, and carried tightly up, and must be absolutely erect. The eyes of moderate size, dark hazel in colour, widely placed, with a sharp, bright, intelligent expression. The muzzle should not be too long, but powerful, and gradually tapering towards the nose. The nose, roof of mouth, and pads of feet distinctly black in colour.

Colour.—Pure white; any other colour objectionable.

Coat.—Very important, and seldom seen to perfection; must be double-coated. The outer coat consists of hard hair, about 2in. long, and free from curl. The under coat, which resembles fur, is short, soft, and close. Open coats are objectionable.

Size.—Dogs to weigh from 14lb. to 18lb., and bitches from 12lb. to 16lb., and measure from 8in. to 12in. at the shoulder.

Skull.—Should not be too narrow, being in proportion to the powerful jaw, not too long, slightly domed, and gradually tapering to the eyes, between which there should be a slight indentation or stop, eyebrows heavy, head and neck thickly coated with hair.

Eyes.—Widely set apart, medium in size, dark hazel in colour, slightly sunk in the head, sharp and intelligent, which, looking from under the heavy eyebrows, give a piercing look. Full eyes and also light-coloured eyes are very objectionable.

Muzzle.—Should be nearly equal in length to the rest of the skull, powerful and gradually tapering towards the nose, which should be fairly wide. The jaws level and powerful, the teeth square or evenly met, well set and large for the size of the dog. The nose and roof of mouth should be distinctly black in colour.

Ears.—Small, carried erect, but never drop, and should be carried tightly up, terminating in a sharp point. The hair of the ears should be short, smooth (velvety), and they should not be cut. The ears should be free from any fringe at the top. Round, pointed, broad, and large ears are very objectionable, also ears too heavily covered with hair.

Neck.—Muscular and nicely set on sloping shoulders.

Chest.—Very deep, with breadth in proportion to the size of the dog.

Body.—Compact, straight back, ribs deep and well arched in the upper half of rib, presenting a flattish side appearance, loins broad and strong, hindquarters strong, muscular, and wide across the top.

Legs and Feet.—Both fore and hind legs should be short and muscular. The shoulder-blades should be comparatively broad, and well-sloped backwards. The points of the shoulder-blades should be closely knitted into the backbone, so that very little movement of them should be noticeable when the dog is walking. The elbow should be close in to the body both when moving or standing, thus causing the fore-leg to be well placed in under the shoulder. The fore-legs should be straight and thickly covered with short, hard hair. The hind-legs should be short and sinewy. The thighs very muscular and not too wide apart. The hocks bent and well set in under the body, so as to be fairly close to each other either when standing, walking, or trotting. The fore-feet are larger than the hind ones, are round, proportionate in size, strong, thickly padded, and covered with short hard hair. The hind-feet are smaller and thickly padded. The under surface of the pads of feet and all the nails should be distinctly black in colour. Cow hocks detract from the general appearance. Straight or weak hocks, both kinds, are undesirable, and should be guarded against.

Tail.—Five or six inches long, covered with hard hairs, no feather, as straight as possible, carried gaily, but not curled over back. A long tail is objectionable.

Movement.—Should be free, straight, and easy all round. In front the leg should be freely extended forward by the shoulder. The hind movement should be free, strong, and close. The hocks should be freely flexed and drawn close in under the body, so that when moving off the foot the body is thrown or pushed forward with some force. Stiff, stilty movement behind is very objectionable.

THE IRISH TERRIER.

The Coming of the Breed.

INDISPUTABLE authority may be quoted for the existence of this Terrier in Ireland many generations ere it became popular in this country. For all that, there are quite a large number who simply regard the variety as one evolved in the "seventies." As a matter of fact, the latter period marked an epoch in Irish Terrier history, for it was in 1875 that the breed was first provided with a separate classification in Great Britain. The dogs at the early exhibitions, although they exhibited more or less affinity to a type, were nevertheless lacking in many essentials, and, viewed through latter-day spectacles, they would probably be voted a "scratch pack." Still, there was the breed in the making, and one could not expect from the homogeneous elements that were scattered over Ireland to produce even an approximation to a perfect whole. The Irish Terrier as it existed in its native land prior to being taken in hand by breeders in this country was just a hard-biting game Terrier, with a variable kind of jacket, sometimes of a deep red colour and of hard texture and at others quite light and soft. Gradually an interest in the breed was created, and thanks mainly to enthusiasts like the late Mr. "Billy" Graham and Mr. G. R. Krehl, Mr. C. J. Barnett, Mr. J. J. Pim, and a few others, it was well sustained. The formation of the Irish Terrier Club in the year 1879 also marked a period in the history of the breed, and since that day it has practically never looked back. At the time of writing it is one of the most popular of all breeds, and the high-water mark of its popularity has yet to be reached. As with all breeds of dogs which have been suddenly thrust into fame, there have not been wanting detractors—men who because of the success that followed it were only too ready to put their finger upon any weak place—but it may truthfully be stated to have successfully weathered the stormy waters through which it passed in the process of evolution.

Perhaps the most critical period in the history of this remarkable little dog was that immediately following upon the

An excellent type of Irish Terrier, Champion Breda Muddler.

abolition of cropping in 1888, prior to which the cruel practice prevailed. Practically all the breeds that were affected by the cropping edict languished to such an extent that for a time they looked like disappearing from the lists of British dogs, while even to the present day some of them have not only never recovered therefrom, but are gradually going from bad to worse. To the lasting credit of the Irish Terrier Club be it said that they were the first body to drive a nail into the coffin of cropping. Instead, however, of the Irish Terrier being adversely affected it seemed to take a new lease of life after cropping had ceased, and at the present day it is second only in regard to popularity to the Fox-Terrier. What enthusiasts have chiefly to guard against is so altering the appearance of the dog that it is nothing more than a red Fox-Terrier.

There seems to be a very prevalent notion existing among novices that there are two kinds of Irish Terriers—the wire-haired dog that we know so well and a smooth. Why there should be such a widely-distributed and absolutely errone-ous impression abroad it is difficult to conceive; but if anyone has any doubt as to its existence all that he has to do is to scan carefully the answers to correspondents in the various papers giving place to kennel matters. Of course, now and again there are sports from the original type in all breeds, no matter how ancient they may be, and it is therefore likely that this fact is largely responsible for the belief to which reference has been made above.

As is the case with all breeds in whose history there are distinctively marked epochs, there are, as it were, associated with such periods individual dogs that by reason of the part they played in connection therewith are worthy of special mention. It is certainly so with the variety under dis-cussion. Were a plébiscite of Irish Terrier fanciers taken as to which two dogs are entitled to be recorded as having most largely influenced the breed in the making it would almost unanimously be conceded that such honour belongs to Champion Erin and Killiney Boy. A little prior to the days of this brace the Irish Terrier was as divergent in type as it well could be; and little wonder, seeing how varied were the strains, each with a certain amount of just claim for consideration, that one found even at shows.

Character and Uses.

" Dare-Devil " is the name bestowed by many upon their favourite Terrier; and if real pluck and a stout heart are anything towards the name, then the Irish Terrier deserves it. Combined therewith the dog also possesses a smart look and a sound constitution, and the Terrier-lover who takes up with the breed for either sport or companionship is not

likely to be disappointed. Unlike some of the breeds dealt
with, the Irish Terrier is not a headstrong variety, game
though he be, and scarcely to be excelled even by the Bull-
Terrier. There is, however, one fault that may be urged
against the dog when used for sporting purposes—namely,
its colour, so difficult to differentiate at a distance from the
environment and often from the quarry when the dog is
in pursuit. On land or in the water the dog is equally at
home, and the excellent thick jacket that the real article
should possess would naturally stand it in good stead. On
account of its hardy constitution this Terrier is one of the
easiest to breed and to rear; while, being a comparatively
small eater, it is not an expensive variety to go in for.

Show Specimens.

We have chiefly dealt with this Terrier on general lines.
When, however, we come to consider it as a show animal we
are at once confronted with the vexed question of trimming.
Now, though it is only fair to state that not all Irish
Terriers require to be trimmed in a wholesale manner,
yet the proportion growing natural coats is so small as
almost to constitute a negligible quantity. What has
been said in respect of trimming the Airedale and the
Wire-Haired Fox-Terrier will apply, with certain individual
modifications, equally to the Irish Terrier. But it would
be manifestly unfair to novices in search of a sire to correct
certain coat defects to pass over the great burning question
because it is unpleasant. How could such a person know
that perhaps the " cracks " in the prize list were prepared as
to coat, and that if allowed to run loose about the house, with
just ordinary grooming, they would grow coats that in length
would not disgrace some sheep?

Choosing a Puppy.

With such a popular breed as the Irish Terrier,
quite a large number of prospective fanciers would not
unnaturally like to know how to select a puppy from the

nest. Such very early choices, however, are always more
or less of a speculation; more especially as at such an age
there are few of those points referred to in the description
to guide one. In that excellent chapter Mr. G. Perry (one
of the most enthusiastic of Irish Terrier fanciers) contributes
to the last edition of Dalziel's "British Dogs," he
says in respect of selecting puppies: "It is far wiser
to leave the selection until after the puppies are some six
months old." Continuing, he says that should selection from
a nest of puppies five or six weeks old be a necessity, then
always pick the one combining, if possible, small eyes
with a good big head, flat skull, plenty of bone, and front
legs that have the appearance of being enlarged at the
joints. The colour at this age should be: Head and legs
a nice yellow-red; chest, neck, and under part of body
lighter—almost fawn—with black hair nearly the whole
width and the entire length of the back from shoulder to
tail. This gradually comes out or is pulled out. Too
much attention should not be paid to colour, and the same
may be said of ear-carriage, until the animal is over teething.
It is the person who seeks to find in a young puppy the
finished appearance of an adult that is so liable to be
deceived.

Description of the Breed.

This dog is fortunate in possessing several excellent
clubs to foster its interests, and the description that follows
is the one drawn up by the parent society, whose foundation
was noticed elsewhere :—

Head.—Long; skull flat, and rather narrow between ears, getting
slightly narrower towards the eye; free from wrinkles; stop hardly
visible except in profile. The jaw must be strong and muscular,
but not too full in the cheek, and of a good punishing length.
There should be a slight falling away below the eye, so as not to
have a greyhound appearance. Hair on face of same description
as on body, but short (about ¼in. long), in appearance almost smooth
and straight; a slight beard is the only longish hair (and it is
only long in comparison with the rest) that is permissible, and that
is characteristic.

Teeth.—Should be strong and level.

Lips.—Not so tight as a Bull-Terrier's, but well fitting, showing through the hair their black lining.

Nose.—Must be black.

Eyes.—A dark hazel colour, small, not prominent, and full of life, fire, and intelligence.

Ears.—Small and V-shaped, of moderate thickness, set well on the head, and dropping forward closely to the cheek. The ear must be free from fringe, and the hair thereon shorter and darker in colour than the body.

Neck.—Should be of a fair length and gradually widening towards the shoulders, well carried, and free from throatiness. There is generally a slight sort of frill visible at each side of the neck, running nearly to the corner of the ear.

Shoulders and Chest.—Shoulders must be fine, long, and sloping well into the back; the chest deep and muscular, but neither full nor wide.

Back and Loin.—Body moderately long; back should be strong and straight, with no appearance of slackness behind the shoulders; the loin broad and powerful and slightly arched; ribs fairly sprung, rather deep than round, and well ribbed back.

Hindquarters.—Should be strong and muscular, the thighs powerful, hocks near the ground, stifles moderately bent.

Stern.—Generally docked; should be free of fringe or feather, but well covered with rough hair, set on pretty high, carried gaily, but not over the back or curled.

Feet and Legs.—Feet should be strong, tolerably round, and moderately small; toes arched, and neither turned out nor in; black toe nails most desirable. Legs moderately long, well set from the shoulders, perfectly straight, with plenty of bone and muscle; the elbows working freely clear of the sides; pasterns short and straight, hardly noticeable. Both fore and hind legs should be moved straight forward when travelling, the stifles not turned outwards, the legs free from feather, and covered, like the head, with as hard a texture of coat as body, but not so long.

Coat.—Hard and wiry, free from softness or silkiness, not so long as to hide the outlines of the body, particularly in the hindquarters, straight and flat, no shagginess, and free from lock or curl.

E

Colour.—Should be "whole coloured," the most preferable
being bright red, red, wheaten, or yellow-red. White sometimes
appears on the chest and feet; it is more objectionable on the latter
than on the chest, as a speck of white on chest is frequently to be
seen in all self-coloured breeds.

Size and Symmetry.—The most desirable weight in show condition is, for a dog 24lb., and for a bitch 22lb. The dog must present an active, lively, lithe, and wiry appearance; lots of substance,
at the same time free from clumsiness, as speed and endurance, as
well as power, are very essential. He must be neither "cloddy
nor cobby," but should be framed on the "lines of speed," showing
a graceful "racing outline."

Temperament.—Dogs that are very game are usually surly or
snappish. The Irish Terrier as a breed is an exception, being
remarkably good tempered, notably so with mankind; it being
admitted, however, that he is perhaps a little too ready to resent
interference on the part of other dogs. There is a heedless, reck-
less pluck about the Irish Terrier which is characteristic, and,
coupled with the headlong dash, blind to all consequences, with
which he rushes at his adversary, has earned for the breed the
proud epithet of "The Dare-Devil." When "off duty" these dogs
are characterised by a quiet, caress-inviting appearance, and when
one sees them endearingly, timidly pushing their heads into their
master's hands, it is difficult to realise that on occasions, at the
"set on," they can prove they have the courage of a lion, and
will fight unto the last breath in their bodies. They develop
an extraordinary devotion for their masters, and have been known
to track them almost incredible distances.

Scale of Points.

POSITIVE POINTS.		NEGATIVE POINTS	
			Minus
Head, Ears, and Expression...	20		
Legs and Feet	15	White Nails, Toes, and Feet...	10
Neck	5	Much White on Chest... ...	10
Shoulders and Chest	10	Dark Shadings on Face ...	5
Back and Loin	5	Mouth Undershot or Cankered	10
Hindquarters and Stern ...	10	Coat Shaggy, Curly, or Soft...	10
Coat	15	Uneven in Colour	5
Colour	10		
Size and Symmetry	10		
Total ...	100	Total ...	50

HOUSING.

The Kennel and its Environment.

Soil.—Quite the most important detail in the successful management of a kennel of dogs, or, for that matter, of one dog that is required to pass a very large proportion of its life outside the house, is the selection of a site for the kennel. No dog can thrive in damp, dark, and draughty quarters or in those where neither bright sunshine nor air can penetrate. Let, therefore, the Terrier-owner consider carefully the site for his proposed kennel, no matter what its size or shape may be. We know that, with a very large proportion of dog-keepers, it is almost a case of Hobson's choice. In such cases, and where only one dog or, at most, a brace is kept, they may be allowed to pass a good deal of their time in the house, though they should always be allowed out regularly for exercise. As the aim of this book is to cater alike for the one-dog man and the more aspiring individual anxious to keep a team for show purposes, the respective interests will have to be carefully considered. Then, again, all the Terrier group are not equally hardy. Breeds like the Yorkshire, the Toy Black-and-Tan Terrier, &c., have to be specially catered for when kept in numbers, otherwise if treated like their hardier relatives dire results would follow.

For any kennel the question of soil is of paramount importance, and there can be very little doubt that a gravelly or a sandy soil is the best, as a clay one is the worst, on which kennels can be erected. On either of the former wet soon disappears; but on the latter, with even the most careful drainage, there is always a coldness and a sodden condition that are inimical to dog-life, and, sooner or later, rheumatism and even worse ailments assert themselves.

Site.—This is of scarcely less importance, more especially in the case of Terriers that by nature are scantily clad—the Bull-Terrier, for instance. In any case, however, a southern aspect, all things considered, is the best; for even if it be very sunny in the hottest weather, yet sunshine is life- and health-giving, and death on many microbes; while it is quite easy, with very simple contrivances, to provide shade during the hottest part of any day. In winter it is that the value of such a site is most apparent, as then it is that sunshine in this country is especially valuable. Still, even though it may not be possible always to select a site with such an aspect as the one suggested, it should be possible always to guard against a draughty situation for the kennel. Should the ground slope gently naturally, all the better, as the objectionable matters may be more readily dealt with than if it were perfectly on the flat. The question of drainage must also be considered; and if the ground be of such a nature that it is at all retentive of moisture, surface drains should be made. Nor is it only the ground on which the kennel itself stands that needs to be considered. In every properly-constructed kennel there should be a yard, or a run, and provision for this should, of course, be made.

Flooring.—As in fine weather ordinarily healthy dogs would naturally pass a good deal of their life outside the kennel proper, it is most essential that the floor material be not only non-absorbent, but warm, or rheumatic troubles will prove of frequent occurrence, with all their liability to recur. Opinions differ markedly as regards the most suitable material for the flooring of sleeping-house and run or yard. The first material that would naturally occur to the average dog-owner would be bricks; but from their porous and absorbent nature they are about the most unsuitable. Concrete floors have many admirers, and in their favour it may be said that they are easily laid, readily cleansed, and non-absorbent. It is, however, a moot point whether they are not objectionable on the score of the dampness that they seem to engender. Ordinary asphalt is too warm in summer, and is also not very durable, being affected by heat and severe frosts. So far as our own experience goes, the most likely material to answer the requirements of dog-owners is the Cork Pavement as made by the British Cork Asphalt Co., Ltd. Apparently this is made from bitumen, cork, &c., is non-absorbent, sanitary, and easily cleaned, while from its very nature it is warm. It is, moreover, easily "laid." Whatever be the final choice in respect of flooring, it must be laid so that there is a gradual slope to an efficiently-trapped drain if no such slope exists naturally. But the great majority of owners have to consider expense, and, therefore, something less high-priced may have to be chosen. A handy-man, used to the laying of concrete, could readily make a most substantial flooring at a comparatively small outlay of time and material.

The Kennels.

Whether these consist of an ordinary portable structure or a range of kennels, it will be found money well invested to go to a firm of repute for them. Firms that make the work of kennel-construction a feature have all sorts of labour-saving appliances in connection with their workshops, and they are thus able to place the finished article upon the market at a less cost than would be entailed in having such a structure made at home. Moreover, the purchased kennels possess features that the average carpenter, amateur or professional, would be scarcely likely to include except under supervision; and it is in these essentials that they score heavily over the home-made erections. Firms like Boulton and Paul, of Norwich, Spratt's Patent, Fenchurch Street, E.C., and Barnard, Bishop, and Barnards, Norfolk Iron Works, Norwich, have for years catered for the dog-

keeper, and their kennels may very fairly claim to be
excellent in every way.

Though the actual kennel, or kennels, will have to be
determined by the number of dogs kept, yet even the one-dog
man ought not to be unaware of the benefits of a "yard."
By the employment of such an addition the chain may be
dispensed with, and thus a most objectionable practice

Range of Lean-to Kennels (Boulton and Paul).

will be discountenanced.   Probably more young dogs are
crippled by the senseless use of a chain than by any other
means; while animals that are so restricted are often spoilt
as regards their temperament.

As we are going largely on the assumption that whatever
kennels are needed will be purchased ready-made, it may
seem unnecessary to enter into the details of construction
that should be arranged for.   Nevertheless, as the cost
of a ready-made kennel might prove prohibitive to many,
it will be as well to remind the amateur maker that

every kennel should be provided with a sleeping-bench, raised some few inches (4in. will be ample) from the floor, otherwise the occupant will be subject to ground draughts, and suffer in consequence, and there should be a day as well as a night sleeping-bench, the latter being fastened up when not in use. Light being very important, a window should be found in every range of kennels. Ventilation should be from the top. Where a range of kennels is contemplated it should never be forgotten to have a passage-way some 3ft. wide the whole length of the kennels, with a door communicating with each compartment. An excellent range is the one illustrated, and made by Boulton and Paul. This shows the general principle that we would enunciate, and also the way the yards are constructed. The only thing that we could suggest by way of improvement is the affixing at the bottom of the railing of a piece of wood, 1ft. or so high, to shelter the dogs, when lying upon the floor, from ground winds. Where one cannot run to kennel railing for dividing off each compartment, a very good substitute may be found in chicken-wire arranged on uprights.

An excellent kennel and run is made by the well-known firm of Spratt's Patent, and is of the lean-to type. It is a very portable structure, and decidedly cheap. Where, however, one contemplates going in for breeding, the Double Terrier Kennel and Run that Boulton and Paul manufacture may be named as well worth consideration. This is readily put together, and embodies all the best ideas in kennel-construction, being comfortable, light, well ventilated, and roomy. With most of the kennels on the market the weak point is the roof, this, as a rule, being of corrugated iron, which is hot in summer and cold in winter unless there be an inside lining of wood. A wooden roof, well built and treated with one of the preparations that prevent "rot," would, we think, be preferable; while better still if it could be managed would be a thatched one.

In addition to the kennels proper, there should be

provided an emergency building or kennels to be employed
in the isolation of any sick patient calling therefor; while
any dog needing constant attention would be better
accommodated indoors.   Even the biggest Terrier would
not be much in the way at such a time, and it would be
far preferable to have the dog ready at hand, where every
attention could be bestowed upon it, than for it to be outside.

For even the one-dog man a kennel is an absolute necessity
if the dog is to pass a portion of its time outside; and
that the majority of Terriers are better kept under such
conditions admits of little doubt.   The firms named
cater most satisfactorily for the small dog-keeper, and there
is little to choose between the products of the best makers.
Still, portability and ease of access for cleaning purposes
must never be lost sight of, combined, of course, with those
other essentials—light, air, and ventilation—referred to in
connection with the more pretentious structures.   No
kennel should rest absolutely upon the ground if it is
required to have a fairly long life.   For a few shillings
small baulks of timber that have been creosoted may be
purchased, and on these the kennel should be stood, so
that plenty of air can circulate beneath.   Neglect of this
precaution means a very short life for any average kennel.

Some owners may not consider it desirable to purchase
a kennel at all, preferring to allow the Terrier, of whatever
breed, to sleep inside.   From the security point of view this
is always desirable.   Still, even when kept indoors at night,
a basket or other sleeping-place out of the way of ground
draughts should be provided for the dog.   This may have
enclosed bedding, or, what is better still, perhaps, if
expense is not a particular object, a Petanelle Rug, as sold
by Spratt's Patent.

It should be scarcely necessary to remark that kennels,
no matter of what type, require to be cleansed periodically,
using Izal or some similarly good preparation and thoroughly
hot water.   This is an insecticide, a deodorant, and a
disinfectant in one, and, therefore, eminently desirable

where an owner wishes to keep his dog under ideal
conditions as regards health. Where there has been an
outbreak of disease of an infectious nature, or the occupants
of the kennel have suffered from either internal or external
parasites, it is incumbent upon an owner to see that the
kennel is treated in the way we have already suggested. In
fact, to make assurance doubly sure, it should be sprayed
with the insecticide, or even fumigated, using one of
the candles as made by Sanitas. Carbolic acid is also
a most useful disinfectant and insecticide. Whatever
preparation, however, is employed, it is advisable not only
to allow the kennel that has been treated therewith
thoroughly to dry before the dog is returned thereto, but
also to allow it to be exposed well to the air. Chinosol is
another first-class disinfectant.

Next to the provision of a sanitary, roomy kennel comes
that of a comfortable bed. To that end the actual
material chosen must be carefully considered. Oat, rye,
or wheat straw, when procurable, makes an excellent bed;
but barley straw awns are very irritating, and this, to
delicate-skinned dogs, is a great disadvantage. Some
varieties need to be especially catered for in the matter
of bedding material, the Yorkshire, the Skye, and
the Clydesdale Terriers all falling within that category.
For all these the bedding, whether consisting of Elastene
(a most useful substance), paper, or other material, must
be encased. It also needs periodically to be changed,
shaken up, and beaten, as dust is a great enemy if allowed
to collect in the coats of long-haired dogs. So far as
the bedding for the average hardy outdoor dog is concerned,
it needs to be changed once a week; while each day the
soiled portions, if any, should be removed. All bedding
requires to be well exposed to the sun and air as often
as possible. Apart from the bedding materials already
referred to, there are others that are occasionally employed—
hay, sawdust (where there are long-coated dogs), pine
shavings, dried bracken, and peat-moss litter. The first-

named is a very dusty material, and the others are
poor substitutes for oat or rye straw; while peat-moss litter
has the additional disadvantage, in the case of a white or
light-coloured dog, that it discolours the coat.

Although, generally speaking, collars and chains are
best dispensed with, yet they must be regarded as necessary
evils, and, whether the Terriers be required simply as
companions or for the dual purpose of watchdogs and for
show, both collars and chains will be required. Suffice it
to say that no young dog should be chained, as it
undoubtedly tends to pull the animal out of shape. For
all that, it is necessary quite early in life to accustom the
Terrier to both restrictive agents. This is best accomplished
by allowing them to be placed on for a short time each day,
at first letting the chain drag. When a little later on the
dog is taken out, a chain may be introduced in order further
to familiarise him therewith. For shows there is a regulation
pattern chain, provided with spring-hooks, swivel, and two
rings to prevent twisting. These may be obtained from
makers of dog-fanciers' appliances.

Where it is out of the question to provide a run (as
advocated) for a companion or a yard Terrier, chaining is
a necessity. This may be done with a minimum of injury
so long as a stop-link dog-kennel spring (Spratt's Patent)
is provided. This appliance consists of an expansion
ring, $1\frac{1}{4}$in. in diameter and 6in. long, with a loop and a
ring at each end. Should the dog make a sudden rush
forward, the spring will gradually expand, and the strain
that would necessarily result without such an aid is
relieved. The stop-link is fastened by means of one of
the rings to the kennel. Terrier collars are made by many
firms, round ones being best for long-coated breeds, as they
do not rub off the coat in the neck vicinity as a flat one
would.

FEEDING AND FOODS.

FEEDING.

Principles of Rational Feeding.

VAST as is the number of people interested in dog-keeping, it must be admitted that but a comparatively infinitesimal proportion of them have even the remotest idea of how their canine charges should be fed. This is not a mere conjectural statement, but one based upon a thirty years' experience of the requirements of the average dog-owner as reflected in the columns of one of the oldest and most influential newspapers giving place to kennel matters, and of a dog-keeper for a still longer period. Indeed, we are prepared further to state that nine-tenths of what may be classed as preventable ills in the dog are due to a misconception of the principles that govern feeding, and that it constitutes the crux alike with the amateur and the more experienced owner. Why this should be so after so many years' sound teaching is, to say the least, more or less incomprehensible; but that it is so must be patent to those who have taken time seriously to consider the question of feeding in its relation to health. Far too many people owning dogs simply as companions and for the more utilitarian purpose of guarding the house and grounds are apt to regard them as receptacles for the consumption of certain waste matters, be they animal or vegetable. That prior to domestication the dog was a scavenger admits of no doubt; but in its altered circumstances it is not so, and to be treated, therefore, as if it were and yet not allowed to lead the more natural life that it enjoyed in the feral state is to impose upon it a task that its constitution is quite unequal to. Little wonder, therefore, is it

if, when a dog is fed under such conditions, Nature after
a time rebels, and shows this unmistakably in the skin and
coat more particularly, digestive troubles, constipation,
diarrhœa, and in various other ways with which the dog-
owner must be only too familiar.

In considering the question of feeding, the most important points are: Is the dog a young puppy (just over
weaning), a more mature puppy of from four to six months
or even older, or an adult? Further, there is the
question of work or exercise in the case of an adult. To
feed all dogs alike irrespective of the life they lead is to
court failure ; for, obviously, with a dog that is worked hard
or exercised freely the waste of tissue is correspondingly
greater than in the pampered animal allowed to lead a life
of luxurious ease before the kitchen or drawing-room fire or
in a cosy arm-chair.

Scarcely less important in its bearing upon the subject is
the season, or the conditions under which a dog is to be kept.
For instance, in winter the food must partake of a more
warmth-giving nature than in the summer if the bodily heat
is to be maintained ; while a dog that is kept outside as a
guard will need food of a kind better calculated to supply
heat than its more fortunate relative that is allowed to sleep
inside. Both these are phases of a subject that must receive
adequate attention if feeding is to be on rational lines, and
certainly no other is likely to give satisfactory results.

Thus far we have considered our subject mainly in
relation to an adult animal whose bodily development is
complete. There is yet to be considered the more difficult
side, namely, that applying to puppies, from the time that
they are usually fit to leave the dam—at seven weeks old
or a little more—up to the time that they are adult—at twelve
months. There are two widely-different schools of thought
in connection with the rearing of young puppies : one is in
favour of a farinaceous dietary until such times as the puppies have attained the age of six months, and to this school
meat is anathema ; the other is an advocate of allowing meat

to enter into the dietary from the earliest times. Though at one time we were strong adherents to the former, yet the experiences of the last few years have shaken our belief somewhat in regard thereto. To-day we incline to the opinion that it is better for the dog-breeder to steer a middle course as being the one more likely to achieve the end he has in view—the building up of a healthy framework. This is only to be done by the use of judiciously-compounded foods, aided perhaps by one of the various substances that science has proved of incalculable service in producing a framework that is all-sufficient for the needs of a healthy animal. For this reason some breeders—and rightly—freely advocate the use of phosphate of calcium in certain foods; while others swear by Plasmon, or something similar, as providing the necessary earthy matters that are likely to produce bone of the right quality to withstand the weight that the body imposes for instance on the legs. It is here where the man who feeds his dog on a more or less scientific system scores over his less well-informed brother who thinks that, so long as a puppy feeds well on the foods provided and has a more or less plump appearance, all is well. The one who supplies a well-balanced food that is readily assimilated seldom or never has puppies deformed by rickets; the other is constantly in trouble therewith. In dealing, therefore, with the subject we will endeavour to keep this end in view. There is, however, nothing hard and fast about this, and the intelligent owner will soon learn so to regulate the various foods that they will accord with the condition of individuals at the different stages of their life.

Lastly, there are the invalid, the stud-dog, and the brood bitch to be taken into account. Naturally an animal that has suffered from some debilitating form of disease will require to have the body attuned. There are numbers of excellent prepared and other foods that may be readily taken that are calculated steadily to repair any inordinate demands that have been made upon the bodily substance of any individual. These we will also refer to when dealing

with what is certainly a complex subject when viewed in the
rational manner that it undoubtedly should be.

It will be patent to anyone on a moment's consideration
that the stud-dog and the brood bitch have at times exceptional drains upon their system.   These, as far as possible, must be met with foods of a kind most likely to
replace the waste of tissue that has taken place.   So far
as the stud-dog is concerned, we strongly believe in giving
him plenty of food that is readily and quickly assimilated.
Finely cut-up raw meat is of great service to him, and should
be always furnished.   Still, it must not be forgotten that
to over-feed such a dog is even worse than to under-feed,
as it is calculated to neutralise his procreative powers.   So
far as the brood bitch is concerned, she must be generously
fed the whole time she is in whelp, as she has not only
her own bodily system to maintain at the correct standard,
but also to nourish the puppies in embryo.   It is here
proposed to enumerate those foods that are best suited to
the needs of adults, and afterwards, when treating of rearing, those likelier to be productive of a healthy puppy
frame.

Vessels.

The care bestowed upon all food-vessels is well repaid.
On no account should food be left standing from one
mealtime to another in the same vessels, no matter of what
they are composed.   Cleanliness in respect of these will
be the means of preventing many a minor disorder.   Even in
the selection of food-vessels it is well to exercise discrimination.   Spratt's Patent, Boulton and Paul, Taylor, and many
other firms catering for the various phases of the fancy sell
first-class non-upsettable food-vessels.   Though not of such
importance as food, yet even the water-supply must be
good, or trouble will be in store for dog and owner alike.
Opinions differ as to whether dogs should be allowed a
constant supply of fresh water or not.   We strongly incline
to the former, and have never found our dogs any the
worse for it.   The water-vessels must be kept as scrupu-

lously clean as the food-vessels, and should be so positioned that they are not readily fouled.

Regularity and Number of Meals.

Dogs should be fed with as much regard to regularity as ourselves : long fasts followed by great feasts are extremely harmful. No Terrier in robust health requires more than two meals a day—the first a light one in the early morning, and the last a much more substantial affair at midday in the case of a house- or a watch-dog, and in the evening where the animal is kept more or less as an ornament.

FOODS.

Meat.

There can be no possible question that the dog is by nature carnivorous : his dentition at once places that beyond the realm of doubt; but it would be a most ill-advised proceeding to feed him entirely on a meat dietary. Equally injudicious would it be to depend solely upon a farinaceous or other dietary. What, therefore, is best is so to combine the one with the other that the resultant food is a fairly well-balanced one. Meat is the most highly concentrated of any dog food, and may be given in many forms—horseflesh being unquestionably the cheapest at present on the market. Nor is there any objection to be raised against it because it is horseflesh : the objection is where the flesh has been obtained from some diseased animal, or one on whom drugs have been plentifully used. Good horseflesh, however, is obtainable, and in appearance should be as readily detected as good beef. If, therefore, when preparing the meal the meat either looks or smells unpleasant it should be at once rejected. It is the greatest mistake in the world to allow a dog to partake of tainted food of any kind.

Where there are but one or two dogs one can rely upon getting the coarser parts of fresh beef from the butcher—

the shin, for instance; in the case of a kennel of Terriers that would be a far too costly proceeding. Throttles and other offal parts also provide change meat-food; but they do not contain the same amount of nutriment as the beef or horseflesh already referred to. Paunches when cleaned, cooked, and cut up form a fairly cheap and readily-assimilated meat-food; but we are not believers in giving either as they come fresh from the cow or the sheep, as some advocate. Bullocks' heads and sheep's heads must also be enumerated as providing meat and some good liquor in which to boil meal or rice, making a thick pudding-like mass.

A question that will naturally arise is, Should food be given raw or cooked? Generally speaking, it is far safer to feed cooked meat to dogs than to allow them to have it raw. For all that, raw *lean* meat, either finely minced or scraped off, is a most nutritious and sustaining food; while in emergencies it will be taken when nothing else will. Fat meat, save in exceptional cases—*e.g.*, when a dog like a Toy Black-and-Tan Terrier shows signs of coat bareness, or in cases of rickets or wasting—should not be given. Even then probably such cases would be better met by judicious doses of cod-liver oil. Liver, either raw or cooked, so much vaunted, we do not believe in *as a food;* as a reward after a lesson or as an inducement for a dog to show himself properly a little liver boiled and afterwards baked may be recommended. Meat should always be placed in boiling water, but should never be fed to a dog hot.

Fish.

We cannot, of course, regard fish as a natural dog food, but we nevertheless consider that certain Terriers are the better for an occasional fish feed, sleek-coated ones in particular. Any of the coarser fish will do, so long as they are carefully freed from bones; but much cheaper and equally appreciated are cods' heads boiled until all the bones are soft and chalky. The liquor is useful for pouring over meals or rice, to which it imparts a flavour. It must, however, not be forgotten that fish has not the same sustaining power as meat, bulk for bulk.

Biscuits and Meals.

These seem to fall naturally under the same heading. For the majority of dogs they constitute the chief foods, and, if well chosen as to make, they constitute most useful and convenient ones to be given in change with others and also in conjunction therewith. Meals, for instance, may be made into a " pudding," as for hounds, and if any of the cooked meats already referred to are mixed therewith this may be given with advantage. Oatmeal is one of the meals very largely employed, but as a rule, being of a somewhat heating nature, it should only be used in winter. Hound-meals like Rackham's, Spratt's Terrier Meal, Rodnim, and similar preparations are better all round. Melox Food is another excellent change-food of the hound-meal type; it is easily prepared and readily assimilated. Meat-meal, as made by Brand and Co., has excellent feeding value, and should be given with softened biscuit or stale brown bread, or even with the hound-meals.

So far as biscuits themselves are concerned, these fulfil a double purpose when given dry—they sustain and act as tooth-cleansers; while from their very nature they tend to the secretion of certain juices that are valuable aids to the proper assimilation of the foods. For the morning feed there is nothing better than dry biscuit. As all biscuits are not of equal food-value it is very necessary to select them with discrimination. Spratt's Patent, Clarke, and Walker and Harrison are three of many well-known firms whose products may be confidently relied upon. All biscuits should be broken up whether they are given dry or soaked. There are most useful biscuit-breakers upon the market that will prove excellent labour-savers where there are many mouths to feed.

Milk.

Though primarily of use in the feeding of young animals, yet milk will often be taken by aged and invalid

F

dogs when more solid foods are refused. We shall treat
more specifically of this and such preparations as are made
therefrom when dealing with puppy-rearing. Lactol as made
by Sherley and Co., and Malt-Milk Food by Spratt's Patent,
are both excellent in their way.

Bones.

From time immemorial bones as food have been
associated with the dog. They should always be provided,
and though they should never consist of splintery pieces or
the bones of game, poultry, and the like, they should not,
on the contrary, be too big and hard. A Terrier with a good
mouth should be able to demolish with comparatively little
trouble beef blade-bones and the like. It is, however,
always advisable to give bones after and not as a meal.
Apart from their value as food they assist in keeping the
teeth clean, and in the case of young dogs in the irruption
of the permanent teeth.   Once a week we usually lightly
sprinkle some bones with salt and stand them in a baking-
dish in the oven : this imparts an additional flavour to
them and is much appreciated. While on this subject we
may say that even with soft foods just a slight sprinkling
with salt is good.

Rice.

Thoroughly cooked rice may be regarded as a very
useful food. We usually mix with it some cut-up paunch
or any pieces of meat that are at hand. Thus combined an
excellent and very well-balanced food is made.

Vegetables.

Occasionally it is politic to give a meal of vegetables
to dogs, though they are of little nutrient value, and in
the case of young-animals very liable to cause flatulence.
Still a little cooked cabbage, spinach, onion, turnip, &c.,
have a gently laxative effect, and where Terriers are kept
up rather close act beneficially if not too often given. They
may be cooked with the meat or in the liquor that ham or

bacon has previously been cooked in. Onions we find act beneficially alike on bowels and kidneys.

Invalid Foods.

. What may be termed invalid foods for dogs are extremely numerous. Among the more valuable are Malt-Milk Food, Lactol, Mellin's Food, Benger's Food, raw eggs, Brand's Extract of Meat, milk with addition of Plasmon, cod liver oil (this especially in cases where there is great waste of flesh), Bovril, milk puddings, and scraped raw lean meat.

Prepared Foods.

Reference has already been made to some of the more generally employed " prepared foods " ; still, there are some few that to the ordinary dog-owner are more or less unknown. Take, for instance, the preparation known as Rackham's Dactyla, which contains, besides starch and albumen, dried dates. Liquid Meat (Kreochyle) is a food that may be given alike to ordinary dog and invalid, and especially where there is any difficulty in connection with the digestion of the ordinary foods.

Aged Dogs.

These require to be treated somewhat differently from the majority in respect of their food, and it is often very difficult to keep in health some old favourite which, for sentimental reasons, it is desired to possess as long as possible. Being unable to take much exercise, there is comparatively little waste. of tissue. Generally speaking, the food should be of a light but nutritious and easily digested kind. Meat should be given in change, and where the idea of giving cooked paunch is not cared for, tripe makes a first-class substitute for an old dog. Milk puddings, a few cooked vegetables covered with a little gravy (but from which all fat has been removed), broken-up biscuits, first softened by means of hot water and then similarly covered

F 2

with gravy, and well-boiled rice, also covered with gravy, are all good for aged dogs. Unless carefully dieted the liver gets deranged, and the whole portal system is thrown out of gear. Naturally, the skin participates and gets into a very irritable condition. Temporary relief may be given by means of Izal in solution (one tablespoonful to a quart of water) which may be dabbed on to the irritable parts.

Unless the liver is working satisfactorily, it may get enlarged, and fits ensue. These are painful to witness, though the dog often recovers from them very quickly. We should recommend as treatment in such cases a mild purge, and also a dose of bromide of potassium (5gr.) three times a day. Old dogs must not be kennelled outside, as they are very prone to rheumatism and to bronchitis and asthma. On the other hand they should not be " coddled " by being allowed to pass their time in front of the fire. Each day a little exercise suited to the individual should be given, and the bowels carefully watched to see that they are acting. If the above instructions are carried out, and fatty meats, very starchy foods (potatoes for instance), pastry, and sugar are disallowed, a dog may live to quite a patriarchal age without causing much anxiety to his owner.

EXERCISING, GROOMING, and SHOW PREPARATION.

A General Consideration.

In the above we have three highly important phases of kennel management—so important, in fact, that no sane owner can afford to ignore them. Indeed, it may be said that on judicious exercise and proper grooming depend very largely not only the health and happiness of any dog, but—what is of paramount importance—his ability for either the field or the home, for one of which purposes, or even for both, the bulk of Terriers are kept. So far as show preparation is concerned, this applies to a far fewer number of dogs than exercising and grooming, but nevertheless it has always to be seriously considered by the owner of show stock, as upon the manner in which a dog is prepared may depend the making or the marring, at any rate for a time, of an individual. Or it may have a greater and more far-reaching influence—namely, whether a profit or a loss is to be shown at the end of the financial year, should it be necessary to run the establishment on paying lines.

We will take the three details seriatim in the order in which they occur, beginning with

EXERCISING.

Its Nature.

Terriers, as will have been gathered from the descriptions which have preceded this practical matter, are a very miscellaneous section. Obviously, therefore, where there are so many differently-constituted varieties, it will at once be patent that one form of exercise will not be suitable for all.

A Yorkshire, a Clydesdale, or even a toy Black-and-Tan
Terrier would of necessity have to lead a life very different
from that of any of the hardier varieties; and as, when
dealing with the many breeds that go to make up this section,
we have described the details of management specific to a
particular variety, all that we need trouble about here are the
hardier members of the group.

At the outset, therefore, we will assume that a certain
amount of exercise is a practical necessity for all the hardier
Terriers, and this irrespective of weather. The chief point
for consideration is of what shall this exercise consist. For
the average Terrier in health and condition there is nothing
like good walking exercise upon the road, with now and
again a gallop across some springy turf, and an occasional
jump over fences, not too high to overtax his powers.
Still, all individuals of one variety even must not be exercised
alike, as constitutions differ markedly, and what would be
health-giving to one might prove prejudicial to another. The
governing factor in all must be a study of the individuals
comprising a kennel. Of course, where there is only one
dog concerned, the task of finding out just the amount of
exercise required should not be difficult. In every case,
however, individual condition must be the chief determining
factor, more especially if the exercise is part of a programme
to be gone through with a view to fitting the animal for a
certain event on a given day.

Judicious road exercise will keep the feet and the legs
in that nice condition beloved of the exhibitor, and no
other method of exercise will have a similarly beneficial
effect. The jumping over slight obstacles, more especially in
the case of a young dog, will tend to that proper development
of the loins that is not to be obtained in any other way.
Greyhound fanciers know its value and practise it religiously,
but many Terrier-men seem to be unaware of its great influence on the symmetry of the young and growing animal.

We need scarcely say that, although Terriers are frequently
exercised behind cycles and even motors (!), yet such a

violent form is calculated to injure rather than to improve the dog so treated. Indeed, we might go further and state that unless great care be taken, it is an act of unjustifiable cruelty. A Terrier may be allowed to trot behind a cob or a horse so long as the pace is not too hot or the distance too great ; but we should not recommend even that comparatively mild form of exercise as a regular thing, and especially to be condemned is the sudden introduction of a dog to a form of exercise to which previously it has never been accustomed.

Amount and Time.

No hard-and-fast rule can be laid down in respect of the amount of exercise Terriers generally require ; it is largely a question to be decided of the individual. Personally, ten miles a day we should regard as nothing out of the way for the average Terrier in health ; and we have proved that he can do that distance with ease year in year out without showing anything but favourable symptoms—a healthy body and an excellent appetite. The writer's own Terriers will do twenty miles over rough country on any day, and then readily respond to the go-out signal in the evening.

Now as to the time for the exercise to be given. This will depend largely upon the season of the year. Except in winter, the early morning is the best time to exercise Terriers generally, so long as there is no meal given just after they return. Dogs, like their owners, are better for a rest before eating, and this we always endeavour to give. It is an act of gross cruelty to give a dog a big feed and then suddenly to call upon the animal to undertake exercise, and is certainly asking for trouble. A reasonable time should always be allowed to elapse between the giving of a meal and the exercise. For that reason exercise is largely dependent upon the time the heavy meal is provided.

Brood bitches will require to be treated somewhat differently as regards exercise during the last stages of their pregnancy, and we shall refer specifically thereto when treating that part of our subject. Show dogs may take plenty of outdoor exercise with great advantage, the chief thing being to see that exhaustion does not follow.

Regularity in the matter of exercise is as important as in the matter of feeding. No Terrier should be exercised by fits and starts : there should be a regular time for that as for any other detail of management. There are times when, of course, it is imperative to keep a dog at home, but as soon as these are past the Terrier should gradually be allowed to return to the old ways as regards regularity of exercise. Apart, too, from the exercise that all Terriers should have, every dog kept in the house at night or even in a kennel should be allowed out for a quarter of an hour the first thing in the morning, again at midday, and the last thing at night. To keep dogs chained to a kennel for hours at a stretch, as is sometimes done, is the refinement of cruelty and stupidity.

What may be termed the pet varieties of Terriers require exercise altogether different from that meted out to their hardier relatives—the Toy Black-and-Tan Terrier, the Yorkshire Terrier, or the Clydesdale, for example. Frequently a day or more will elapse before weather favourable to outdoor exercise for such breeds will supervene. Still, this should not prevent them from being exercised indoors by means of a ball or similar plaything, which will tend to keep them in decent condition. Whenever the weather will allow of exercise being taken outside, it is, of course, better than the suggested indoor substitute. In the case of wet weather it will be found an excellent plan thoroughly to dry the feet of any toy dogs allowed to exercise under such conditions. To do so may savour of coddling, but experience has shown that it is the correct thing. Further, we would say that sparsely-clad Terriers should wear a coat when allowed outside during very cold and cutting winds. Bull-Terriers, English White Terriers, and Black-and-Tan Terriers all feel severe weather unless they are properly looked after in the matter of a coat.

We have not dealt with the question of exercise for

puppies. This is considered in the section devoted to Breeding and Rearing. Our remarks so far have been confined to adults.

GROOMING.

Practically every domesticated animal is the better for attention being paid to its jacket, and so far as show dogs are concerned the process of brushing and combing is absolutely necessary if the dogs are to stand any chance against those with whom they are brought in friendly rivalry. We have already dealt with the subject of grooming hard-coated dogs when treating of the Airedale Terrier, and of the long-coated ones under Yorkshire Terriers and Skye Terriers respectively. There is therefore no necessity again to go over the ground. Suffice it to say that for all hard-coated Terriers the familiar slanting-bristled brush, as illustrated in the Airedale chapter of " English and Welsh Terriers," and the type of brush shown under Yorkshire Terriers in the same book, are those most in favour with fanciers generally.

There is yet another group of Terriers that call for slightly different treatment from that meted out to the hard-coated or wire-haired or the long-coated varieties. We refer to the smooth-coated, of which the Bull-Terrier and the Black-and-Tan Terrier are types. These should, of course, be brushed daily, but they are best finished off with a hound glove or a chamois leather in the case of Black-and-Tan Terriers, or by vigorous hand-rubbing in that of Bull-Terriers. The chamois leather helps to add lustre to the coat of the one, and the hand-rubbing, while improving the texture of the coat of the other, is productive of muscular development.

When and How Performed.

Grooming, to be of real use in stimulating the skin and thus tending to the production of a good coat, should be begun quite early in the life of a puppy, of course using a brush suited to the tender skin of the animal. Practically,

say, from the age of three months the puppy should be
groomed each day, the actual amount . received depending
upon the age of the dog and the condition of the coat.   From
a quarter of an hour to half an hour each day may be very
well spent upon the brushing and combing of any adult
dog ; and many fanciers go to the extent of a second and
even a third brushing where the case seems to stand in
need of it.   The great thing to remember is never to groom
upon a full meal, and to be as regular in connection with the
detail as with those of exercise and feeding.   Constant
grooming should tend to improve considerably the personal
appearance of any dog, to keep at bay objectionable external
parasites, and, lastly, to the promotion of a healthy skin
action.

The Broken-haired Terriers require a special form of
comb ; this was illustrated in the section dealing with
" English and Welsh Terriers."   Such combs are sold by
fanciers' providers like Taylor, of Bradford, Spratt's Patent
(Fenchurch Street), and others.   These combs will remove
all the dead coat, thus giving the new coat proper opportunity
for developing, and generally help to give the jacket that
smart appearance that should obtain more especially with
a dog intended for the show-ring.   Here we would emphasise
the fact that all combings should at once be burnt, as frequently on such may be found the "nits" or egg-cases of
dog-lice, which in due course would hatch out and probably
the insects would infest the dog again.   The amount of
combing that a dog will require will be entirely regulated by
the jacket, and this varies naturally with the season of the
year, and a little with the conditions under which the animal
has been kept.   Generally speaking, a dog kept outside the
year through will grow a thicker and a longer coat than one
kept indoors, and a slightly harder one.

Washing.

One of the points in connection with grooming that the
average novice owner requires enlightening upon is washing.

A frequent question is : How often should I wash my
Terrier? To this we would answer, Only when absolutely
necessary in the case of a show dog—usually a few days in
advance of the date of the fixture at which the animal is
entered. This applies more particularly to breeds which
exhibits signs of soiled coat very quickly—white ones, or
those in which white predominates as a ground-colour. If,
however, the ordinary hardy Terrier is brushed and combed
each day, and has its coat occasionally treated to an insecticide, washing need not often be resorted to.

When it is necessary, care should be taken to use a soap
that is suited to the purpose. Soaps that are too strongly
alkaline have a deteriorating effect, as they rob the jacket of
the lustre and life which are necessary in the case of a show
dog. There are excellent soaps in the market, and some of
them are to be found advertised. At any rate we can speak
from experience of Garstin's, Spratt's, Newton Chambers',
Naldire's, Rackham's; while if a shampoo wash is preferred
(as it sometimes is), then Sherley's and Spratt's are alike
to be recommended. Quite recently, too, there has been
placed upon the market a preparation of this nature, known
as Canicura, that is most excellent as a cleanser and an
insecticide combined.

The water used for washing a dog should be pleasantly
warm. A very good test is to bare the elbow and put this in,
and if it can be easily borne the water is fit. The body
and legs should be washed first, and the head left to the last.
Every care must be taken to keep soap, &c., out of both eyes
and ears, and the latter should be thoroughly dried by
" dabbing " them with cotton-wool rolled round the pointed
end of a wooden penholder. As the production of a flat coat
is aimed at in most Terriers, it is most undesirable to allow
a dog after washing to be returned to his kennel in a half-
dried state. He must be thoroughly dried, and the combing
and brushing should be continued until the " lay " of the
coat is as it should be. Nothing is so conducive to a " curl "
in the coat as inattention to this point. For a similar reason

a dog should not be allowed to swim and then return to a
kennel to finish the drying process.   This should be com-
pleted, on his reaching home, in the same way as suggested
after washing.   Where, too, a dog is allowed to bathe in the
sea (a questionable thing with show dogs), he should always
be rinsed with soft water on arriving home, otherwise there
is a danger of the coat becoming matted.

SHOW PREPARATION.

Trimming.

Really, show preparation proper is comprehended under
feeding, exercising, and grooming, as ordinarily understood.
Outside these, however, as we have shown when dealing with
the various breeds, there is much to be done that no amount
of book instruction can teach.   For instance, to trim or not
to trim is a question that must be asked when about to
prepare almost any Terrier for show; but that it is
necessary, if not desirable, must be patent to anyone who has
eyes to see, when surveying a group of Terriers at any show
worthy of the name.   It is not proposed here to attempt to
teach the trimmer's art, even if it were possible : this must
be acquired by experience, often bought rather dearly, and
most difficult to carry out without a mentor.   When dealing
with a team of broken-haired show Terriers it is almost impossible to dispense with the service of the " professional," for
apart from the skill required to keep within the very narrow
border-line that separates "trimming" which is "winked at"
and "faking" which is punishable there is the question of
time involved.   Of late years *the* show preparation of many
popular breeds of Terriers has resolved itself into a feat of
hairdressing so cleverly performed that it is often difficult
to say by what manner of means the result has been achieved.
The Kennel Club has, it is true, printed some very
intelligent and intelligible rules for the guidance presumably
of those who do not know ; but we must confess that anyone
who is not purblind at a show must see that labour-saving
cutting appliances are often used in the preparation of some

exhibits, for in no other way could such a uniform result be achieved. Time was, and that not so very long ago, when finger and thumb, aided by resin, were deemed all-sufficient for smartening up an individual dog whose coat exceeded the regulation length of the fancier. It has been found that a far quicker process exists, and though not, perhaps, practised in a wholesale manner, it nevertheless obtains. We have tried what can be done in the direction named, and have satisfied ourselves that, judiciously performed, it would at any cursory examination " pass." For all that, we do not think such devices tend to enhance the reputation of dog-showing. Legitimate trimming and smartening up should be properly defined, as it is tacitly allowed, and when it is exceeded those responsible should be treated like those transgressing in other directions. The subject is always an unsavoury one, and, like the poor, is always with us. As we have stated when treating of the different breeds, the amount of trimming required varies with the individual. Some dogs require practically none; while others require a course of preparation in the " moulting-room," as it is facetiously dubbed, calculated to make old-time fanciers turn in their graves. We have seen dogs subjected to the process " before " and " after," and all we can say is that they are frequently so changed that many must, at times, have a difficulty in recognising their own.

Of late years it is much to be regretted that more labour-saving appliances than stripping-combs and finger-and-thumb have been employed in the preparation of many varieties of Terriers. We refer to the " clippers " made much on the same principle as those employed on the beard. These, if carefully used three weeks or so before a show, enable the coat to be made of the length beloved of the fancy. According to the laws that be such aids to preparation are inadmissible; but the difficulty lies in the detection. If some of the Terriers that have thus been operated upon are closely examined, more especially at the junction of head and neck, a ridge that is left there

will be more or less noticeable.   For the face these clippers
appear to answer well, and are used right up under the
ears with the idea of improving head-length.   The whole
business of show-preparation in connection with the majority
of Terriers is more or less unsavoury and bristles with difficulties ; but it is necessary to refer specifically to many of
these in order to give the novice some little idea of what he
will have to combat before he can hope to compete and win.

Handling.

In this we have a perfectly legitimate operation, and one
that every owner of a show dog should do his level best to
value at its true worth.   Far too many novices seem to think
that their charges require no preliminary rehearsal of the
show-ring business, and are astonished, when leading their
dogs into the ring, to see them absolutely scared by the
scene that confronts them.   Not so the " old hands " which
have been carefully prepared weeks in advance properly to
comport themselves when placed side by side with those with
which they are being brought into friendly rivalry.   We have
more than once seen excellent specimens " go down " before
undoubted inferiors, owing to the fact that the ones had
not been trained and the others had.   It is no fault of the
judges, who usually have, especially with popular breeds and
one-day shows, very arduous tasks to perform.   Such men
and women can hardly be expected to take up their time
with a business that should have been rehearsed weeks in
advance.

Where possible, prospective exhibitors should endeavour to
get a few friends with their dogs and gradually teach their
unshown charges to " show " themselves under the varying
conditions and distractions which obtain at all exhibitions.
This may be done by a short lesson and a small reward once
or twice during school.   Nothing that is calculated to add
to the difficulties of perhaps already nervous dogs must be
allowed.   On the contrary, every encouragement must be
given to get them to show themselves on the day required.

Some highly-bred dogs are by nature nervous, and the capable handler or old-hand exhibitor will at once recognise this and treat his charges accordingly. Long ere the actual show-ring business has to be rehearsed, every dog should be accustomed to both collar and chain. This may sound comparatively insignificant advice, but the truth of it will soon dawn upon those who expect to show their dogs without familiarising them with the preliminaries referred to. Novices should note carefully the way that professional handlers go about their business, and take a leaf out of their book.

BREEDING AND REARING.

BREEDING.

Advisability of.

APART from any other considerations, to breed from adult bitches that are constitutionally sound is desirable, if, indeed, it be not absolutely necessary. In the domestic dog, often living a life of luxurious ease, it is Nature's method of putting to good use certain excess materials that may have accumulated. Thus, bitches which are bred from are far healthier, as a rule, than those which are prevented from exercising their maternal functions, and are not so liable to those common sequelæ lacteal tumours as those that are secluded each time they are in season. Physiologically, therefore, it is without doubt alike sound practice and humane to allow healthy bitches occasionally to breed. We use the word "occasionally" advisedly, for sometimes—usually from monetary considerations—it is the practice of some owners to mate their bitches each time that they are available. The inevitable result of this is that the progeny are weakly and the constitution of the dam is seriously impaired, even if nothing worse happens.

Immature Bitches.

Though of paramount importance, the question as to the best age at which to allow bitches to breed is as often as not left unconsidered. This is a great mistake, as many a young mother is absolutely ruined by being allowed to breed at the very time that she is building up her frame. A moment's reflection should be sufficient to convince anyone of the fallacy of breeding from an immature animal, as two such drains upon the system as the building up of the frame and the nourishment of the fœtus would be going on contemporaneously, to the certain detriment of both. We know that breeding from a bitch at the first time she is available is not only advocated by some writers, but also practised by not a few breeders. Still it is to be condemned, no matter how much it may be advocated. In our opinion the first period of œstrum, as it normally occurs, should always be passed, and even the second one if it should fall at a season of the year when the puppies would not get the necessary amount of sun and open air in which to develop.

Œstrum, or the Period of " Heat."

Œstrum is a natural physiological function that with bitches in a state of domesticity occurs twice in a year, a period of about six months intervening. It is at such times, and such times only, that a bitch can breed. We think it absolutely necessary to make this statement in a manual primarily intended for novices, as we have met with individuals who seem to think that the bitch is always available. Œstrum may occur for the first time in young animals at any period after the six months, but generally speaking from the seventh to the tenth month would represent the normal. Naturally, with such a great functional disturbance occurring there are often changes of both habits and temperament some little time in advance of the actual change. First it will be observed that a bitch is extremely thirsty, and there is a tendency to frequent micturitions, the quantity passed at any time being small. Still more noticeable are the changes in the habits of the bitch : she is restless to a degree, sometimes giving utterance to peculiar whines, difficult to translate, but none the less marked ; while not infrequently the whole temperament undergoes a radical change, a mild-mannered bitch evincing a disposition to " snap." As, too, the disturbance reaches its height there are other outward signs that will at once suggest to the least practical that something is amiss. The generative parts will gradually commence to swell, redden, and eventually there will be a discharge,

G

whitish at first, but afterwards reddish, the colour increasing in intensity until blood alone is passed. Isolation of the bitch must at once take place, and preferably she should be placed in a lock-up kennel, stable, or outhouse, or a misalliance will assuredly take place. When it is proposed to breed from her, *the* time for her to visit the prospective sire is immediately after the red discharge has ceased. If the parts in the vicinity of the generative organs are lightly touched, the bitch, if she is ready, will stand quite still and move the tail, carried gaily, in a very significant fashion.

Although bitches ordinarily are in season only twice in the year, cases are known where they have shown symptoms of such a disturbance thrice or more in such a period. Generally speaking these are what are known as " false heats " ; they are characterised in much the same way as the others, but the bitch absolutely refuses the male, and is, moreover, very bad-tempered, snapping and snarling viciously whenever he approaches.

As a rule the period of heat lasts about three weeks—one week in developing, a week in which it may be said to be at its height, and another in which the physiological disturbance gradually passes away, the parts resuming their normal appearance. We have already indicated that feverishness accompanies the ushering-in of the period, and therefore clean fresh water should always be accessible. It is also very advisable to keep the bowels moving freely, chiefly by providing soft foods and those having a cooling influence upon the blood—cooked green vegetables, turnips, onions, and the like—and to provide an altogether lighter dietary than ordinarily.

Where a bitch is not required to breed, it is usually desirable to get rid of the milk-like fluid that is always secreted, whether she has access to the male or not, and neglect of such a precaution may result in one of those unsightly and often painful lacteal tumours so frequently seen in bitches not allowed to exercise their maternal functions. This may be done by gently rubbing the parts in the vicinity of the teats with camphorated oil and by giving twice a day 1dr. of Epsom salts and 10gr. of bicarbonate of soda in water. The secretion referred to may be looked for towards the end of the period when the bitch, had she been served, would be due to whelp.

Gestation Period.

Normally the period of gestation in bitches is sixty-three days, but sometimes this is exceeded, at others not reached. There is nothing absolutely hard-and-fast in this respect. Taking Terriers generally, however, we should say that nine weeks would be about the average. Where this average period is not reached is with more or less coddled and highly-fed small varieties. There are few indications, even to the experienced eye, of a bitch being in whelp until after the middle period of gestation, when the teats will usually be more prominent. We say usually, as there are cases where bitches alter very little here and yet by the proportions assumed elsewhere there are unmistakable evidences of their being in whelp. Where, therefore the teats do not seem to develop well, an effort should be made to assist Nature by gently manipulating them, or even by drawing them down by means of a breast-exhauster. If this detail be not attended to, when the whelps attempt to suck they will not be able to do so, and may succumb before a foster-bitch can be requisitioned. Notwithstanding the fact that there are some who believe in a theory that the sex of the whelps may be determined beforehand, this has no foundation in fact.

Fundamental Principles.

So far we have been chiefly dealing with certain more or less fixed phenomena, and though to bring about the breeder's desiderata we shall have to consider certain natural laws—heredity and selection—they will exhibit a greater tendency to variability. Before, therefore, entering into the substance of these, it will first be desirable to get rid of some of the fallacies that invariably beset the path of the novice breeder. First it may be stated that there is no royal road

to the scientific breeding of any animal, and therefore the
novice must at the outset disabuse his mind of the very
erroneous belief that the faults of generations of breeding can
be checked by any quick-change process.   To give an
example of what is meant.   It is a very common belief that,
given a comparatively ordinary bitch, by mating her to
a sire excelling where she is deficient her faults are
thereby at once corrected in the progeny.   If the laws governing breeding could be reduced to such a rule-of-thumb practice, the process would, of course, be simplicity in the
extreme; but they cannot, as we shall show as we proceed.
Breeding is an art, and as much thought and care must be
bestowed upon it as upon any other art, if the best results are
to be achieved.

Another very common error is to suppose that a pedigree
animal is necessarily good as an individual.   As a matter of
fact there are thousands of pedigree dogs and bitches that
are not worth the annual licence paid for them.   Pedigree is
an important factor in breeding, but it does not of itself
confer individual good qualities on all the members of any
litter.   To be of value the pedigree must be considered alike
as a whole and as regards its various component parts.   To
the novice many pedigrees are most delusive : they are drawn
up to show a great deal of quality in the remote ancestors
that they include, while the near generations are but
nonentities.   Illustrious ancestors are, of course, required, but
they must be *near* as well as remote ; and the nearer they are,
so long as the blood is of the right sort, the greater the chance
of the breeder obtaining something worthy of the trouble he
has taken.   Stud books, therefore, are most desirable reflexes,
and the breeder with any aspirations should possess them, if
possible.

With each breed of dog that we have discussed there has
been given a description drawn up by experts.   Each description is supposed to represent a standard, and though it is
necessarily ideal rather than real, the efforts of breeders must
be directed to producing animals of a type that as closely as

possible approximates to those standards. These descriptions, therefore, as well as the outward characteristics of dogs that by the places they gain in competitions must necessarily approximate to them, must be kept steadily in mind. There are many breeders who are sufficiently conversant with old-time and present-day blood to know with a fair amount of exactness the best way to correct certain defects or to strengthen any points in their own brood bitches. This only comes of long and careful study over a number of years.

Now as to the brood bitch herself. Elsewhere we have referred to a common fallacy that widely obtains—namely, that almost anything is good enough so long as the sire is good and excels where she is deficient. To follow such a theory could only end in one way—the perpetuation of a race of individuals not worth their keep. We may say once and for all that the dam should be selected with as great care as the sire. She need not be a bitch with a great show career : on the contrary, such bitches by reason of the life they lead are not best suited for the exercise of their maternal functions. She should be the best of her kind procurable as far as her blood and outward characteristics are concerned, she should have youth on her side, be robust as to constitution, and should come of a stock free from hereditary taint, by which we mean that no disease that is likely to be transmitted to the progeny—rickets, for example —should exist.

The part that the biological law of heredity plays in breeding must always be kept steadily in mind. There is scarcely any necessity to define what heredity is so far as the majority are concerned, but for the few we may describe it as a tendency on the part of living beings to transmit certain characteristics to their descendants. Connected very closely therewith—indeed, forming an integral part thereof—are other factors that must not be lost sight of : atavism and pre-potency. As is fairly well known, the former is a disposition to revert to some remote ancestor rather than to an immediate one ; while the latter is the power of individuals to stamp their progeny with their own characteristics, no matter what other influences are exerted by the family as a whole. A knowledge, therefore, of such laws and their methods of application should be of the greatest value to the breeder when founding a kennel of show dogs.

We have next to consider the vexed question of in-breeding. Every breeder of stock upon scientific lines is agreed as to the value of this in producing that fixity of type which is desirable, as he is also agreed as to the harm that may be done by carrying the principle to excess. If we consult the pedigrees of dogs as given in the stud books and elsewhere, we shall find that consanguineous breeding is largely practised. Some aver, Never breed closer than father to daughter and mother to son; but occasionally still closer breeding is practised in order to retain desirable characteristics. There are no hard-and-fast rules to guide the breeder how close he may go without transgressing Nature's laws with respect to the lower animals. Each individual will be a law unto himself. It may, however, be asserted as a principle that directly there is weakness either of intellect or of constitution in-breeding should be at once discontinued.

Given, therefore, a soundly-constitutioned bitch of excellent lineage, the next question to be dealt with is, " How shall she be mated ? " We have already indicated the general principles on which selection should depend; but now we must be more specific. Her pedigree must be carefully considered alike as regards the strong points and the weak ones, and the effort must be to select a sire that not only himself excels but whose strain excels where she and her family tree reflect weakness, having due regard to those factors of heredity—atavism and prepotency. This will at once suggest to the practical mind the absurdity of using a sire that is good-looking by accident even though he may be a champion of champions. He is simply one of Nature's sports, and should be severely left alone no matter how extensive his prize-winnings or alluring his appearance. " Blood will tell " is an old and very true adage, but the blood to tell must be on both sides in something like a corresponding ratio. We have known more than one aspirant to breeding honours thus to fail.

Next we have to discuss two or three points that are material to the whole question of breeding. One of these is the sending of the bitch to the sire. On no account should a breeder, with a view to saving expense and trouble, attempt to keep a stud-dog; for it is scarcely likely that the dog would " nick " with all the matrons in a kennel. Again, considering the fact that all the best blood in the country is available on the payment of a reasonable fee, the absurdity of the thing should be apparent. Unless a breeder can accompany a bitch (and this is always desirable in the case of a nervous, highly-strung individual), she should be carefully placed in one of the hampers that dog appliance makers sell, and due notice be given of her despatch. It is not advisable to feed her at least for half a day prior to the visit, and no outside aid is needed, or indeed desirable, as a general rule. On her return from the visit she should be kept thoroughly quiet for a few days, and afterwards fed and otherwise treated as if nothing out of the way had happened, until after the fifth or sixth week. Still, throughout her period, having regard to the demands upon her system, she should be more generously fed than ordinarily. Then it will be necessary to restrict her somewhat in the matter of exercise, and, of course, she should not be allowed to over-exert herself in any way by fast running, excitement in the chase, or jumping. About the middle period it is a good thing to administer a vermifuge; and a fortnight before she is due to whelp she should be introduced to her quarters and allowed to go there for a short time each day. She will make her bed in her own particular way, and this may safely be left to her. A week before the event she should not have any bones, and soft food only should be given. The bowels should be regular, and it is not advisable to give any purgative except under the advice of a veterinary surgeon. Healthy bitches seldom require any help from man, and are, in fact, best left

alone, though where a bitch has been made a companion of
she usually likes her master or her mistress to be present.
Terriers, as a rule, are strongly constitutioned; but in the case
of valuable dogs it is always advisable to arrange for a
foster-bitch beforehand, as the milk-supply sometimes dries
up quite unexpectedly after a week or so, and the business of
hand-rearing is such a difficult and risky one that it should
not be relied upon.

One other point in connection with the brood bitch needs
to be discussed here—the influence of a previous sire.   The
fact is that, with every precaution, some misalliances will
occur in the best regulated of kennels.   Ere now we have
known valuable bitches destroyed on the assumption that
they would be useless ever after for producing pure-bred
progeny.   No greater fallacy could be entertained.   That
mongrel alliances are objectionable leaves no room for doubt;
but records of telegony, so far as they exist, go unmistakably
to show that such alliances do not unfit the bitch for producing
pure-bred progeny in the future.

When buying bitches wherewith to found a strain, the
novice breeder often hesitates between purchasing a maiden
and one which has proved her worth as a dam.   Really there
is little room for doubt between what is a known and an
unknown quantity, and his choice should always lie with
bitches which have already shown proof of their ability to
reproduce their kind.

The Sire.

There are one or two points in connection with the
sire that call for notice.   First, as to his selection.   Broadly
we have suggested elsewhere the lines on which the prospective breeder should select his stock; and what has been said
in respect of the brood bitch holds good equally of the stud-
dog.   Family excellence as reflected in the pedigree must be
the true guide when selecting a mate for a bitch.   Generally
speaking it is a far easier matter to obtain this in the sire than
in the dam, whose family excellences are often not manifested

until the third or even the fourth generation. We of course refer to the stock that often is placed on the open market and therefore readiest to the hand of the breeder. When going to a breeder of repute or buying with a set object in view, the case is quite different. So far as the sire is concerned, he must be of individual excellence, and his family tree should moreover reflect that excellence throughout and not merely in the remote generations. He must be free from any hereditary tendency to transmit disease, or any objectionable peculiarities—a " butterfly " nose for example. He must be vigorous, not too much used (" popular " is the usual term), and his record at the stud be a good one. If the bitch is getting on in years, then the sire should be correspondingly young, and *vice versa*. Two aged animals are not likely to produce first-class progeny.

REARING.

The Nursing Mother.

We left the brood bitch at a point when she was about to become a mother, and we are here assuming that the event which has caused the breeder some weeks of anxiety has come off, and that his efforts now must be directed towards the offspring as well as the mother. Naturally, after giving birth to whelps, the bitch will be the first consideration once it has been found that the puppies are warm, comfortable, and sucking freely. Not only has her strength to be maintained, but there is some leeway in that direction to make up. Her food, for a time, must consist of slops. An excellent food after parturition consists of well-boiled arrowroot and milk, which, while being sustaining, has also a soothing influence. She will not care to move from her whelps, even for natural purposes, for several hours after the event. However, on the second day she will probably show a disposition to go out. Advantage should be taken of this to remove the very soiled parts of the bedding, replacing it with fresh, but nothing must be done to cause her undue anxiety, or this may have an injurious effect on the milk-flow. Sheep's-head broth, from which every particle of fat should be removed, may be given, slightly warmed. Care, however, must be taken to see that she has no food likely to react on the puppies (causing diarrhœa) or foods of too watery a nature, otherwise she may have an excess of milk. For this reason, assuming that the bitch is strong and well, she should gradually be allowed to return to her normal dietary after the second or, at most, the third day. In about a fortnight, however, there will come a great drain upon her natural resources in the form of stored food, and this must be met by more liberal feeding. She should be fed on the little-and-often principle, and the greatest care observed in regard to the cleanliness of the food-vessels. At the age of three weeks assistance should be given the mother by allowing the puppies to feed. They will, of course, make a very poor hand at lapping at first ; but if their noses are gently directed to the food which has been prepared they will quickly learn, and this will relieve the dam considerably.

Food for Young Puppies.

Of late years science has come to the aid of the dog-breeder and provided him with food that at any rate approximates very closely to that of the mother. Formerly the dog-rearer had to depend almost entirely on cows' milk, which is a very poor substitute for that of the bitch, being deficient alike in fat and proteid content. In Spratt's Malt Milk Food and Sherley's Lactol, however, we have two preparations that fulfil all the requirements, and on one or other of these the breeder should rely until weaning-time, coupled, of course, with the dam's milk. Full directions for their use will be found with each tin of the food. Other excellent foods for the purpose in hand are Benger's and Mellin's. With the quartet named no breeder ought to have any difficulty in rearing puppies that were strong at birth.

The most trying time in the life of any puppy is just after weaning—say at the age of seven weeks. Too early weaning is to be deprecated, as puppies need not only the dam's milk, but also the warmth that her body affords. We have not dealt with those minor operations—docking, in those breeds in which Fashion has decreed that operation to be necessary, and the removal of dew claws in all breeds. These were referred to in the section treating of " English and Welsh Terriers." Still we may just say that both should be performed during the first week of a puppy's life.

Weaning-Time.

For reasons already given we do not think that any puppy should be weaned until about the seventh week. It is then that the great test of proper nutritious food begins to exert its influence. Lactol or Spratt's Malt Milk Food should form the staple dietary until the third month. Six meals a day, at regular intervals, should be afforded, the first meal being given as early as possible in the morning and the last one quite late in the evening. After the tenth week farinaceous foods may well enter into the dietary—such as stale bread and milk, oatmeal and the best wheat flour in equal parts, mixed with milk and cooked until it is of a stiffish consistence. Only sufficient for a meal should be put into the feeding-vessel, which must be thoroughly cleansed afterwards and put away until again required. Nothing approaching sourness must be allowed, and therefore it is better to make all foods in small quantities, even though the trouble be greater. Those responsible for the looking after of the whelps must see that each puppy gets its rightful share of the food, as often a very strong and greedy puppy will take advantage of the weaker members of the litter.

At the end of the third month four meals a day should suffice, and Melox Food, Puppy Rodnim, and broken, softened puppy biscuit may be allowed in change. In addition to these and other staple foods, finely minced cooked tripe may be given in very small quantities to each puppy. A little later minced raw meat may be introduced with advantage twice or thrice a week. As the permanent teeth begin to replace the milk teeth, dry, broken puppy biscuits will be appreciated. For any puppies that show signs of weakness a little Plasmon (as directed by the makers) may be given in the soft food. By the time the sixth month is reached three meals a day, as varied as possible, should be given, and this number may be continued until the puppy is an adult. Necessarily, too, a greater proportion of finely cut up cooked lean meat may be employed. Generally speaking vegetables are not good for young puppies, as they tend to produce a flatulent condition. Still, now and again they may be allowed, especially onions, beet, parsnips, and green vegetables. These may be mixed into a pudding-like mass in the cooked meal. Potatoes, in quantity, are not good for dogs, whether puppies or adults. In the case of show-dogs where a clean-cut jaw is much admired, many breeders eschew the use of bones, as they tend to cheek-development. More especially is this inadvisable in the case of Bull-Terriers.

For feeding adults the reader is referred to the chapter " Foods and Feeding."

Where there is not the convenience for keeping a number of puppies on the premises, the majority should be drafted out to " walk " in couples, as suggested in the case of Fox Terriers in " English and Welsh Terriers." This minimises considerably the risk from infectious and contagious diseases, and it is, generally speaking, good for the puppies so treated, so long as the " walker " understands his business.

Teething.

Closely connected with this phase of our subject is Teething, a process that often causes puppies some consider-able discomfort and pain. It is also something more than a local disturbance affecting the mouth : the whole system is more or less disorganised. For this reason many fanciers do not pay so much attention to irregular ear and tail carriage if they are prior to the process being complete as they would do were either carried indifferently after the permanent teeth, or the majority of them, were irrupted. The adult dog has forty-two teeth—twelve incisors, for cutting; four canines, or fangs; and twenty-six molars (twelve in the upper and fourteen in the lower jaw), adapted for grinding. The permanent teeth are irrupted at from the third or fourth to the seventh month.

As a good level mouth is much valued in all Terriers, the breeder should watch carefully the puppy's teeth. Sometimes the milk-teeth are not shed while the permanent ones are advancing, and if the former are not removed there is a prospect of a bad mouth. A veterinary surgeon's aid is occasionally necessary to remove such teeth. We have found it a good plan to give very occasionally a minute dose of calomel in the soft food while puppies are shedding their teeth. Our own plan is to give just as much as will lie on the tip of an ordinary penknife blade.

TRAINING.

WHETHER kept purely as companions and house-dogs or for the more important duties that by nature the majority, at any rate, of the Terriers are fitted, they should most certainly be trained. An untrained dog is, generally speaking, a public nuisance and a source of trouble and anxiety to his owner. And here it may be well to mention the fact that should a dog, while in the charge of a servant, do any damage to domestic stock or inflict any injury upon man it is the owner and not the servant who is responsible. It seems advisable to mention this, as many owners do not realise that they are liable for the dog's acts while in the charge of their servants.

The old adage that " manners maketh man " will apply with equal force to the dog, and a dog that has been trained, if only in house-manners, is in our opinion ten times as valuable as the unfortunate animal on whose home or other training not one hour has been spent. Generally speaking, when the average man rears a litter of whelps to a saleable age he thinks that his responsibility ceases, and he takes no further trouble in the matter. Not so the individual who takes a keen delight in his charges : he (or she) believes in turning them out so that they are a credit not only to the rearer, but to the family to which they belong. In these days of cycling and motoring it is more than ever incumbent on dog-keepers so to train their dogs that they are not sources of danger to the well-ordered public. To horsemen, again, untrained, boisterous, barking dogs are a grave danger, and the sooner owners recognise this the better for themselves and for the public. We have seen more than one serious accident result from such a cause as that referred to, and are, therefore, deeply impressed with the advisability of warning dog-owners as to the risks they run by not keeping their canine charges under proper control. It is one thing to allow a dog to have a bark and a scamper on a field or even a sparsely-used country road, but quite another to tolerate barking and heel-snapping at horses in the streets of a crowded town. As by far the greater number of Terrier-lovers keep dogs purely for the sake of the companionship they afford and the protection that they offer to premises at night, we will deal first with that phase of the subject which concerns them.

Obedience.

First in regard to order of teaching and first in importance is the lesson of obedience. On this practically hinges every other lesson that has to be inculcated, even in the higher education of the dog. As soon, therefore, as a puppy is capable of answering to his name this, the first act of obedience, should be instilled. For the first few months of a puppy's life he should be allowed to take matters fairly easy as regards lessons; but as soon as he attains the age of four months, or a little before, he is sufficiently old to be schooled. The lessons, however, must never be long and should always have a pleasant termination—the pupil receiving a tit-bit. The trainer must always endeavour to control his temper, though it must be confessed there will be many occasions on which he will be sorely tried. When teaching a puppy to answer to his name it is always advisable to associate the lesson with a mealtime. The kennel-name should preferably be short, of one syllable in fact, when a very little time will suffice to make the puppy familiar therewith.

This part of the education complete, the trainer may now proceed to get the young animal to follow. At first there will be considerable difficulty, and the lesson must for a time be restricted to one's own premises. Gradually the field of operations should be extended, though before it will be safe to venture out and allow the young animal to make his acquaintance with the larger outside world he must be accustomed to both collar and chain, otherwise were they to be used without any preliminary introduction the trainer would certainly have a bad quarter of an hour.

It may be mentioned that collar and chain are *not* to be used with the object of fastening a young animal to a kennel. This would be a fatal mistake, and only end in disaster to the puppy. The collar and chain are for restrictive purposes, it is true, but only if they are rendered necessary by the puppy's conduct when out for exercise or to get him used to them by the time when he may be required for show purposes. If the collar be put on for a short time each day and the chain be allowed to drag while the puppy goes about the garden or a field in the vicinity he will very soon get accustomed thereto, especially if they be associated with some act of pleasure.

The real difficulty of a trainer begins when the puppy makes that acquaintance with the larger world referred to above. There is probably no more curious creature on earth than a puppy, and it is this curiosity which so sorely tries the temper of the average trainer. Instead of following briskly as he should, the chances are that the puppy will endeavour to investigate everything strange with which he comes in contact, to say nothing of evincing a desire to fraternise with any and every member of the dog community he meets with on his way. Again, unless he be quite different from an average puppy he will have an irresistible desire to travel in an exactly opposite direction to that required, and will, moreover, indulge in one of those scampers so trying to his trainer. Of course, he should be whistled to and an endeavour made to get him to return. The trainer must not, however, attempt to follow unless the puppy gets clean out of sight. He should stand his ground and patiently wait the return of the wanderer. He will come back after a time looking, and no doubt feeling, very sorry for his conduct. On no account must he be beaten, or he will in his puppy mind for ever associate the whacking with the return, and the trouble of the trainer will be increased a hundredfold. Instead of a beating give him a reward. We know this is opposed to the usual practice, but we have found it to answer so well that we have no hesitation in recommending it to others, contrary though it may appear. The worst that should happen to the recalcitrant puppy is that he should have a lead or a light chain attached to his collar and be led the remainder of the way. This plan must be repeated each time he offends, and unless he be particularly wilful a material improvement in his conduct will soon be noticeable. The restrictive agent once removed on the puppy reaching home, the trainer must act as if nothing out of the common had happened.

Respect for Domestic Stock.

The next lesson in obedience will be to instil in the puppy the fact that he must respect such domestic stock as fowls, sheep, and the cattle of the field and the farm. Chevying and worrying domestic stock are, we are sorry to admit, only too prevalent, though Terriers are not as a rule such great offenders as some other breeds. Still, from the first the Terrier must be taught that even the cat must be respected. This can be readily done where a cat forms part of the " family." So far as farmyard and similar stock are concerned, we find it an excellent plan to take the puppy on a lead or a chain where he is likely to come in close contact with such stock. If he shows any disposition to bolt after it he should be sternly repressed and at once pulled up rather smartly by means of the chain. It is in most cases nothing but the desire to scamper after something as a frolic, just as children do. This lesson must be repeated many times, and if after several a desire to chevy is still manifested then it will be well to let him taste a switch across his back just to enforce the lesson. As soon as by his demeanour it is noticed that he passes domestic stock without exhibiting

H

any fondness for " mutton," poultry, or what not, then the
lead may be discontinued.

Another most useful lesson in obedience to enforce and
closely connected with the subject at issue is to make a puppy
walk at heel when told.   To do this the trainer should take
him down a narrow lane or path bounded on either side by
a hedge, and carry with him a light switch. He should then
call the puppy to heel, and should he show any disposition to
come forward the lightest touch on the nose with the switch
will suffice to keep him in position.   Personally, we find if we
carry a stick and put it to the right or to the left when the
puppy comes forward on the one side or the other this is
ample.   Still, individuals differ considerably in respect of the
amount of teaching required to enforce any particular lesson.

House-Manners.

To instil thorough house-manners in any puppy is not
only a work of considerable time, but one entailing a vast
amount of patience.   For all that, it is an absolutely necessary lesson, and therefore must be inculcated at any price.
A dirty dog cannot be tolerated indoors.   From the very
first puppies—that is, from the age of two months and
upwards—should be taught acts of cleanliness.   This is best
brought about either by putting them outside for a short
time on each occasion that they awake from a sleep and
after a meal—assuming, of course, that weather conditions
are favourable and that the breed is a fairly robust one and
the individual puppies are healthy.   Where this is not
the case then some sanitary sawdust should be put in a
shallow box and the puppy placed thereon at such times as we
have indicated. If this be put in an odd corner of a scullery
and kept cleared and the sawdust renewed each day it will
not be at all objectionable.   Especially is it desirable that
young puppies should have access to a receptacle of this
kind the last thing at night, just after the big feed that is
to induce them to sleep the night through.   After about the
sixth month a puppy should be " clean in house," unless

there be something to cause him to offend. Now and again one meets with puppies that cannot seem to be cleanly, no matter what attention be given to them. In all such cases as have come before us they have been due to some trouble needing the veterinary surgeon's care. When, therefore, it is found that, say, a nine-months-old puppy which is given every chance is constantly committing himself it is usually safe to assume that there are physiological conditions to account for it, and the services of a veterinary surgeon should be requisitioned.

When a puppy which is apparently sound continually transgresses he must, of course, have the offence pointed out. No thrashing, however, should be administered, as that tends to intensify rather than to mitigate the trouble, and especially in an ultra-nervous individual. If the offence be pointed out each time, a puppy soon gets to associate the rating therewith, and generally mends his ways—that is, unless he be a kennel-fool, when he should be painlessly destroyed.

Apart, too, from the subject of cleanliness in the house there are other lessons scarcely less important to be instilled. One of these is never to jump up at anyone. Many puppies have a habit of making friends with every Tom, Dick, and Harry. This should not be tolerated for one moment. And especially necessary is it to emphasise the fact that any attempt on the part of a puppy to paw at a friend that his owner may chance to meet must be met with a stern rebuke at least.

Unless absolutely unavoidable or by special request, a dog should never be taken when visiting a friend; and even when this is the case the animal should be left at the door to await his master's return. Here again the services of the trainer will be necessary if the dog is to become perfect in house-manners. The lesson in keeping guard will have to be carefully taught, much after the manner in which a sportsman teaches his field dog to assume a recumbent position until told or signalled to proceed.

Coming under the category of house-manners is the behaviour of a dog at mealtimes. In nine cases out of ten
when a dog is ill-behaved at mealtimes—impatient for food
—it is the fault of the owner or of a member of his family.
This is brought about by making the dog a sort of waste receptacle for any objectionable pieces of meat or indigestible
pastry, or other odds and ends. Thus in process of time
he will have developed positively shocking table-manners—to
say nothing of aldermanic proportions.

As Guards and Protectors.

Very little by way of training is necessary in order
to make of a Terrier a smart house-guard or, as far as
its size will admit, a protector of the person or of property.
It is as natural for a Terrier to be watchful as for a cat to
catch mice. Still there are some Terriers that are dull and
that need a little sharpening of their wits. This is best
brought about by keeping them in the company for a time
of an exceptionally alert dog of any breed. The dullard
and the adept should be kennelled in such a position that a
good view of anyone coming to the house is obtained. This
should very soon have the effect of smartening up the less
alert dog. If, however, after keeping the two dogs together
for a couple of months no appreciable difference is seen it
may reasonably be concluded that the owner has happened
upon that comparative rarity among Terriers—a kennel-fool,
and he should be got rid of.

There is just one other thing that must be taken into
consideration, and that is whether the dog is sound of
hearing. With white breeds of dogs, or dogs in which there
is a preponderance of white, deafness often occurs. Before,
therefore, making a purchase it is always as well to test a dog's
hearing. Congenital deafness is incurable, and, of course,
a dog suffering therefrom is useless from any standpoint.

Puppies begin to show signs of alertness at a very early
age—three months or even sooner. The owner should therefore by the sixth month be able to tell for a certainty whether

this or that dog is likely to be worth keeping, no matter whether it is for show or utility purposes. Quite early, too, in a puppy's career it is well to teach him to "guard" small articles. This accomplishment, of course, may be taught in the house. A puppy should be made to assume a recumbent position and told to guard a tobacco pouch or some similar trifle. The trainer should then pretend to go out of the room, walking backwards. If the slightest attempt on the part of the young animal to leave his post is noticed he should be at once returned to the old position and some words used that are likely to be readily grasped and be significant of the occasion. Directly the dog keeps his guard until the trainer returns the lesson should be discontinued, and a reward should always follow at the end. Once a dog has been taught to remain and watch over small things there will be no difficulty in getting him to look after, say, a bicycle, or a basket, &c.

So far as acting as personal protectors is concerned the majority of Terriers are too small to undertake seriously this important business. There are, however, two—the Airedale and the Bull-Terrier—which are in a slightly different position. These dogs may go to scale at from 45lb. to nearly 50lb., and are therefore capable of rendering good service, the Bull-Terrier especially, which is the most determined and gamest dog for his size that we have met. No man if he has any respect for himself would care to run the risk of an encounter with a 50lb. Bull-Terrier that meant business, especially if the latter has been taught to tackle at the throat. A Bull-Terrier is as agile as a cat, and can readily be taught to fly at the throat. Still, although we have more than once taught Bull-Terriers of our own to do this, we must confess that there have been many occasions when we have had our doubts as to the advisability of it. Once a Bull-Terrier "means business," sticks are not of the slightest avail, and unless a vital part can be reached something undoubtedly very serious happens. It is scarcely necessary to say that such a lesson as we have indicated should be taught with the animal muzzled, and even then it is fraught with risks.

Terriers, to take them generally, instinctively as it were assume the rôle of protector over those whom they have learned to regard as friends. If, therefore, anyone wishes to get on the right side of dog nature we would suggest that he or she attends to the dog personally, feeds, grooms, exercises, and generally ministers to its wants. There need then be very little doubt should occasion arise as to the part the dog would play. A good guard, it is scarcely necessary to say, only gives the alarm when a stranger approaches a house. Directly the stranger is admitted into the house the dog would of course retire. Some people imagine that a good guard is the dog that is so savage that one dare not approach the house. This is a great fallacy, and the man or the woman possessing such an animal is laying up a store of trouble far beyond belief. An intelligent guard dog should have discretionary power, and unless he can differentiate between friend and foe is not worth his keep, to say nothing of the fact that he is a danger and a menace to the well-conducted public.

For Sporting.

Originally Terriers were dogs intended to go to earth to oust from their retreats underground foxes, badgers, and other large vermin. To-day, though they are still employed occasionally for such purposes, yet the majority are kept for other purposes. Needless to say, when Terriers are wanted for such purposes as those named they have not only to be of a certain size, possess undoubted stamina and courage, but they have to undergo a highly specialised training that is really without the scope of a work of this kind. Such training is generally given by the servant of a Hunt, or, in the case of districts where foxhunting as ordinarily understood cannot be followed, by men who have grown up as it were with the business of ousting Reynard from cairns and suchlike places. We do not therefore propose to touch upon the subject beyond saying that, contrary to the frequently-entertained opinion, the mission of Terriers is *not* to kill such quarry as we have referred to, but simply to locate and to bay the quarry in the case of badgers, or to turn them out of their retreats in the case of foxes. Even then the Terriers get badly mauled, more especially those used to badger-earths. The novice must not imagine for one moment that the wonderful badger-dogs that he reads about exist in the flesh: they are paper dogs only. Only those who have been present at a badger-dig can truly appreciate what that animal is like when at close quarters, and frequently a Terrier has a part of its head or jaws snapped off should he have to act on the defensive. A badger will snap a broomstick as easily as a carrot, and we have heard that ere now he has been known actually to splinter iron. At any rate we can testify to his immense jaw power, and we should certainly think twice before allowing any Terrier of ours to try conclusions with one.

Ratting.

There are, however, many ways in which Terriers may be used in sport in which the odds against them are not so great, and in which they are at the same time performing real service to man. We refer to the sport of ratting. Now it has been decreed, and wisely, that the rat is one of the worst of animal pests against which man has to contend. It has also been decreed that Terriers can render excellent service in keeping them down. Still, small comparatively though the rat be, he is no mean antagonist for a young Terrier, and his fighting powers must not be underrated. If, therefore, an owner has a young Terrier which he wishes to try conclusions with a rat he should first make practically certain of his dog's capabilities in that direction. As a rule, to allow such a Terrier to tackle a full-grown rat without being properly entered is, in ninety-nine cases out of a hundred, calculated to spoil for ever and a day that dog's career against a similar quarry. Granted that all Terriers regard rats as their natural enemies, but to tackle them successfully is quite another matter.

Assuming that a puppy comes of a working, game type, there is comparatively little trouble in imparting the knowledge which he requires to set about the rat in a business-like fashion. Such a puppy should have a full mouth, and should be taken a few times to see how an expert dog goes about the work. When the rats have been despatched he should be allowed to mouth and encouraged to worry them, as by such means he gets accustomed to the peculiar smell given off by the rodents. Next he should be introduced to a few live rats in a wire cage and his demeanour carefully noted. If he seems anxious for the fray that will be a good sign. Still he should not be allowed to try just yet. He should see the rats taken out and despatched one by one by the old dog, the while he is held on a lead. If this lesson be repeated once or twice and the puppy still exhibits every inclination to try conclusions he should be accommodated, if possible, with a half-grown rat. Should he kill cleanly and well his wishes should be still further gratified, until in fact his education in that direction may be considered complete.

Perhaps before detailing the information concerning ratting we should have said something in regard to ferrets, as these, in the case of a sporting dog, have to be employed very frequently for both ratting and rabbiting. From the first, therefore, if the Terrier owner keeps ferrets he will be well advised to allow the dog to make the acquaintance of the ferrets. Our own plan is to introduce the dog to the ferrets at feeding-time. This is more readily done when the ferrets are kept in an outhouse on the Court principle than in a hutch. The ferrets would come to whistle or call at mealtimes, and any Terrier that we wish to introduce is taken there on a lead. If the Terrier has previously killed rats, and perhaps a stoat or a weasel as well, he will un-doubtedly evince a disposition to " go for " the ferret. A sharp reproof, " 'Ware ferret," and, if necessary, a switch reminder must follow ; and this lesson must be repeated until the dog's behaviour towards the ferrets is what it should be. Still, when actually at work, more especially with polecat ferrets against rats, it is excusable if now and again a ferret falls a victim to what is after all a natural desire, for a ferret is only a domesticated polecat. Moreover, a polecat ferret approaches so closely in colour that of the quarry that very quick discernment on the part of the dog is called for. We need not enter here into the other details connected with breaking to ferrets, as the ground has already been covered in the writer's little work on " Popular Dog-Keeping."*

Retrieving.

Before finishing with this subject of training a few remarks will be necessary in respect of the part a Terrier is sometimes expected to play—namely, that of a sporting field dog. So far as our experience goes the Terrier, taken generally, is a failure when thus employed unless he is kept for that and nothing else. Nor is the reason far to seek. By nature he is provided with a very powerful jaw, made to cope with vermin, and is what sportsmen term a hard biter. Imagine, therefore, a dog which, say, one day has been employed to kill down perhaps hundreds of rats at the bottom of an old corn rick, a few days after being required to retrieve " tenderly " a bunny that his owner has killed! To do the one he is asked to exercise his natural proclivities to the full; to do the other, suddenly to repress them. The result, generally speaking, is a gigantic failure, and little wonder.

Rabbiting.

As regards rabbit work it is undoubtedly advisable in the case of Terriers to keep them exclusively for this purpose, for reasons already adduced. Terriers are often employed for bustling bunny out of a thick covert and also in conjunction

---

* " Popular Dog-Keeping." By J. Maxtee. Price 1s. 2d., post free, of Mr. L. Upcott Gill, Bazaar Buildings, Drury Lane, W.C.

with ferrets for bolting rabbits from their burrows. For the initial lessons at any rate there is nothing better than the good example set, say, in the case of a puppy by its mother if she be expert at the business. Yet the trainer must not rely absolutely upon that, or the puppy will depend too much upon the expert and as a consequence become a poor tryer. Before taking the puppy out with a view to imparting the necessary lessons it will be desirable to allow the young animal thoroughly to acquaint himself with the smell of a dead rabbit. He should be taught to nose and to wind it, but not to mouth it. Some trainers believe in first introducing the puppy to a live rabbit, but the way we have advocated will be said generally to answer the purpose better. Similarly with respect to the work in connection with rabbit-burrows, the young dog should first be taken to a burrow in order to see how a more experienced one performs the work. The whole business in detail should be gone through in his presence, from the putting in of the ferret to the despatch of the rabbit as it bolts into the net placed for its reception. Dogs are extremely imitative; hence the value of their seeing how a thing is done.

"Watering."

When treating of the various breeds of Terriers mention has been made when any one of these showed exceptional qualities as water-dogs. It will therefore be as well briefly to refer to the method of inculcating the few lessons that may be necessary. The practice of throwing a young dog into the water cannot be too strongly deprecated, as it is calculated to ruin for ever its chances of excelling as a water-dog. Directly the weather is suitable and a puppy is old enough to be trained it may be taken to the water with a view to getting it to enter. If it has been taught to retrieve small objects, all the better. The site chosen should preferably be such that the trainer and his pupil can walk right down to the edge, and, moreover, be shallow. If possible take the puppy to be taught in company with an elder who is already expert, and then throw a small piece of biscuit a few inches from the edge for the youngster to retrieve. If hungry, the chances are that he will endeavour to obtain it. Increase the distance slightly each time he recovers the biscuit, until eventually the puppy ventures beyond his depth and has to swim for it. This lesson will need to be repeated several times before confidence is gained, but once gained it is never lost—at least in our experience. Broken-haired Terriers that are allowed to " water " should always be rubbed thoroughly dry on returning home, as suggested elsewhere.

THE COMMONER AILMENTS AND PARASITES.

By nature Terriers, to take them generally, are a very robust group, and if kept under the conditions advocated in this book they should ordinarily give very little trouble. Still, in kennels where every endeavour is made to preserve the most sanitary conditions, many most troublesome diseases and parasites will occur, calling for prompt action. Often in sparsely populated country districts veterinary surgeons are difficult to obtain; but if the owner is able to render first aid he will at least have done something towards alleviating maybe the pain from which his dog is suffering, or yet again, by prompt action, be the means of staving off a troublesome complication. For such cases this chapter may be useful.

It is absolutely necessary in certain diseases to know the temperature of the animal. In a state of health the dog's temperature is 100 to 101½. When, therefore, this is exceeded, fever is present. The temperature should be taken by means of one of the thermometers sold for the purpose, inserted in the rectum.

Anæmia.

Poorness of blood is a commoner condition among dogs than is popularly supposed. As in the human subject, there is a paleness of the lining of the gums and of the mucous membranes as a whole; while the dog is invariably weak, showing little inclination for exertion of any kind. Sometimes it may arise from a wrong dietary, combined with insanitary surroundings; but oftener its causes are more obscure. If a dog has been largely fed upon a farinaceous dietary it will be found that a little finely cut-up raw lean meat is excellent; while the food generally must be of a nourishing and readily-assimilated character. In cases where there is a marked falling away the services of a veterinary should be at once requisitioned. Blotch or Surfeit, as it is called—characterised by a breaking out into sores—is sometimes due to an anæmic condition, although an overcharged system may produce the same symptoms. Administer 1gr. to 3gr. of reduced iron twice a day in food, or 20 to 40 drops of Easton's Syrup in water night and morning after food.

Blotch.

By dog-owners generally this is regarded as a distinct disease. It is, however, more correctly described as a phase of Eczema in which large sores are a characteristic. Unless prevented, too, patients will lick these in order to get relief, thus intensifying the trouble by exposing a greater flesh surface, which ultimately scabs over. It may be due to a poorness of blood (Anæmia, which *see*), or to an overcharged system due to errors in dietary. When this latter is the case, the bowels must be briskly moved and the dietary carefully regulated. When a dog persists in licking a sore he must be prevented by means of a muzzle with a piece of canvas sewn over the front. The sores themselves must be dressed with boracic acid ointment.

Canker of the Ear.

Three forms of " canker " (so-called) are met with : one due to the presence of a minute parasite (*Symbiotes*) inside the ear; another, also internal, that is often characterised by a disgusting smell, due to the objectionable discharge; and external canker, when the flap of the ear is involved. Dogs affected with canker quickly show it by pawing at the offending part, or holding the head at a peculiar angle indicative of discomfort, and shaking the head, while there are both internal (a redness) and external (inflammation and ulceration) evidences, with a dry, hot, scaly eczematous appearance. For internal canker, Spratt, Bird and Storey, and Sherley all sell excellent preparations; while for external canker the ear must first be carefully cleansed—using warm water and a wine-red solution of Condy's Fluid, or zinc ointment or ointment of balsam of Peru—well dried, and boracic acid ointment applied twice or thrice a day.

So far as internal canker is concerned, pending the sending for the preparations referred to the owner may very well try a gentle syringing with spirits of wine and lukewarm water (1 in 20), afterwards well drying by means of a piece of absorbent wool rolled on the point of a penholder, and gently dabbing the ear, renewing the wool as it becomes soiled or damp, then blowing therein through a quill a little boric acid powder, or equal parts of finely-powdered iodoform and subnitrate of bismuth. Light food and a gentle aperient are also called for.

Chorea, or St. Vitus's Dance.

A well-known nervous affection, in which twitching of the limbs is a very prominent symptom. Though the patient apparently suffers no pain, yet the malady is a most distressing one to watch, and, unfortunately, in ninety-nine cases out of a hundred, remedies are useless. When the disease follows on an attack of distemper, and is severe, it may be regarded as incurable. In comparatively mild cases 20 to 40 drops of Easton's Syrup, given in two tablespoonfuls of water twice a day after food, may afford relief once any feverish symptoms have abated. Veterinary surgeons also prescribe strychnine in very minute doses, but the amateur had better not attempt this. Two to 5 drops of liquor arsenicalis in water, night and morning, has proved beneficial, but it must be given for a considerable time, say for three weeks, then discontinued for ten days and started again. This treatment may be continued for several months, and the diet must always be light and nourishing. In very bad cases the heart is affected.

Constipation.

House-dogs often suffer a good deal from this condition, more especially if the dietary has not been carefully selected. Though an all-sloppy diet is bad, yet equally so is one consisting entirely of dry foods. The happy medium must be hit, and the fæcal discharges should be observed to see that they are normal. If it can possibly be obviated the owner should not resort to drastic purgatives. By using a warm soap-and-water enema the bowels may be so relieved that if proper food and exercise are afterwards given there will not be a recurrence of the trouble. A little raw bullock's liver will act as a gentle laxative, but it has little nutrient value as a food and is not generally to be recommended.

Usually soap-and-water enemas (which should always be introduced tepid) are made on the rough-and-ready principle —by mere guesswork, in fact. There is, however, a correct and an incorrect way of doing this. About 2oz. of dry yellow soap should be cut up into thin slices, and dissolved by pouring thereon about 1 pint of boiling water, and thoroughly stirring. The soap, of course, acts as a slight bowel irritant and the tepid water softens the fæces.

Cough.

By most novices this is regarded as a disease instead of a symptom of many ailments, all of which require to be treated according to the conditions present. Though worms or even indigestion may give rise to a cough, yet one of the commonest causes is a derangement of the respiratory organs or air-passages. It is therefore all-important to diagnose the true cause; for whereas a cough arising from an attack of indigestion or an infestation of worms may be relieved by timely attention to the cause, yet it is not an easy matter for a novice to detect when the lungs or the bronchi are attacked. Still, if accompanying a severe cough there is a considerable rise of temperature, perhaps a viscid expectoration and laboured breathing, the owner may at

least suspect bronchitis and send for the veterinary surgeon
without delay.

Deafness.

As stated when passing in review all-white varieties like
the Bull-Terrier and the English White Terrier, deafness is
very common amongst them, as indeed it is in white animals
generally. Such a condition in any animal discounts its
value considerably, for a deaf dog, as well as being useless
for show, will be absolutely valueless as a guard to property ;
but any dog that shows signs of deafness should not be too
hastily condemned. Frequently, as in the human subject,
the wax-like secretion will be present in such a quantity
as to make the dog "hard of hearing," or even very
deaf. A gentle syringing with lukewarm water will probably give relief if persisted in, care being taken to dry
thoroughly the internal portions after the operation. It is,
however, advisable first to warm some glycerine in a spoon
and drop into the ear a little of this. Deafness less often
arises from growths, when a veterinary surgeon alone can
be expected to afford any relief. Where deafness is con
genital it is of no use keeping the dog.

Diarrhœa.

Alike with adult animals and puppies this is one of the
commonest of all ailments. The causes are numerous, and
many of them to the lay mind are obscure. Still, some of
the commonest may be found in the presence of worms,
distemper, injudicious feeding causing indigestion, the abuse
of purgatives (and especially flowers of sulphur), and
exposure to cold. If neglected, the disease may develop into
dysentery, when the services of a veterinary surgeon must be
obtained. From what has been stated it will at once be
apparent that it is of little use attempting to treat a patient
so suffering without first removing the cause. On no account
must the diarrhœa be too speedily checked, it being Nature's
effort to get rid of the objectionable matter. On the contrary, it will be found beneficial to give a small dose of

castor-oil with a view to hastening the process. Subnitrate of bismuth is a most useful drug to give twice or thrice a day—5gr. to 10gr. given dry upon the back of the tongue will usually afford relief. Where, however, there is considerable pain, opium is frequently employed—5 to 10 drops of tincture of opium in a little water twice or thrice a day. Ten grains to 60gr. of prepared chalk may be added with advantage in the tincture form; but this is best given under professional advice. Equally as important as the use of drugs in cases of diarrhœa is the food : this must consist largely of peptonised milk, or milk and arrowroot. A little raw meat shredded very finely, and mixed with some boiled rice, will prove alike tempting and beneficial. Barley-water is the best drink to provide. It is very necessary to keep the hindquarters clean by means of a long-handled brush dipped in a warm solution of Condy's Fluid. So far as very young puppies are concerned, the treatment should chiefly be through the mother. Give the mother 10gr. of bicarbonate of soda twice or thrice a day in food, combined with careful nursing and a warm, dry bed in a dry, airy kennel. Sometimes a half-teaspoonful of the chalk mixture that any chemist will make up may be given with good results.

Distemper.

Of all dog diseases this is the one in which mortality is the greatest, and it is rightly named the kennel scourge. Despite an enlightened literature, it is noteworthy how comparatively few dog-owners have any correct conception concerning Distemper. A very large number imagine that it is a disease of puppyhood, that one attack renders a dog immune, and that it is absolutely necessary for a dog to be attacked. All this is erroneous and very misleading. One of the peculiar characteristics of the disease is the number of forms it assumes, necessitating widely different treatment. The best means of preventing the disease other than keeping a dog away from centres of infection (not merely the dogs

I

themselves, but also the persons waiting upon such sick animals), are healthy surroundings, proper food, and good exercise. It is the strongly-constitutioned dog that is the nearest to disease-proof ; while the weakling and the wastrel is the most prone to it.

Distemper begins with a running from eyes and nose, a loss of appetite, hot nose and dry tongue, and a rise in temperature. Later, perhaps, a cough is present, with or without diarrhœa, mostly the former. Having removed the patient (which should have a coat provided) to proper quarters, preferably a warm, airy kennel, the discharge from eyes and nose must be kept removed, or complications are likely to ensue. Bird and Storey's Distemper Pills we have found useful in this phase. By prompt treatment the disease may not show any complications. If, however, the lungs or the bronchi, or both, are attacked, which will be evident by the quick breathing and the peculiar " rattle " that is heard in the air-passages, a veterinary surgeon should be called in, as to attempt to treat the dog would be inadvisable in the extreme. When the liver is involved the dog exhibits a yellowness of the mucous membranes, &c., and this phase is known as the " Yellows." Chorea is a common sequel to distemper, and, as stated under its heading, is incurable.

The food is all-important in a case of distemper. Frequently a dog will refuse to eat. In such a case it is usual to give milk, egg, and Bovril (2oz. of milk, half an egg, and a teaspoonful of Bovril), mixed, three or four times a day, with, in addition, a teaspoonful of brandy. An egg should be beaten up in a little milk and given the patient to lap. If it is not consumed, change it often : it must not become sour. Still, if the dog can be induced to take more solid fare, all the better. The liquor from a boiled sheep's head, poured over some stale bread, while intimately mixed therewith, or a portion of the meat removed from the head and finely cut up, makes a nourishing and appetising dish. In cases of great debility or entire refusal of food, give a teaspoonful of Brand's Beef Jelly three or four times a day ; also finely-

minced beef, rolled into boluses and given as pills—two or
three may be given at intervals through the day. Lactol is
a useful food to be given as change in such cases, and so
also is Sanatogen.

Eczema.

Under this heading may be comprehended Blotch and Red
Mange, both of which are really forms of Eczema. By many
owners this blood disease is supposed to be contagious. This
is contrary to fact. That it is hereditary, however, has been
fairly well established. Eczema may be regarded as one of
the commonest of all diseases, and one of the most difficult
to combat. As regards external appearances it has much in
common with Mange proper, and it is therefore a pardonable
error for a layman to be deceived in respect thereof. Practically every part of the body is liable to be attacked, and if
the sores or scabs that form in bad cases be neglected the
dog presents a sorry sight. The disease, like distemper,
presents many phases, for in one case may be noticed
what is popularly called " moist " and in another " dry "
Eczema. The owner must, therefore, be careful to notice
how the dog is affected before attempting home treatment,
otherwise he may readily aggravate instead of alleviate
the condition of the patient.

The average dog-lover, taking an intelligent interest in
his charges, should be able with fair accuracy to tell whether
or not worms, an overcharged system, poorness of blood,
teething, or rheumatism is a probable cause, and to take
measures accordingly ; but there are many other causes that
no one except skilled veterinary surgeons could diagnose.
The fact is Eczema is a most puzzling disease, and it is this
that makes treatment by the novice so doubtful. The
majority of owners finding their charges suffering from
Eczema in nine cases out of ten attempt to treat the effect
rather than the cause ; hence their difficulties are increased.
That the irritation of the skin should be allayed as soon as
possible admits of no doubt ; but the cause must, at the same

* I 2

time, be treated. Such being the case, it will generally be
found safer to seek professional advice than to " tinker "
with remedies whose action upon the particular phase of the
disease in question the lay mind cannot determine. In wet
Eczema, more especially between the toes, boric acid and
starch powder dusted on will prove of great benefit, just as
boric ointment or Bird and Storey's Eczema Ointment will
be found of use in allaying irritation in many simple cases.
Another useful preparation is 1 part of flowers of sulphur
to 6 parts of olive oil.

Fits.

These are extremely common, more especially in puppies
when teething, or when harbouring worms. Such fits are then
termed Convulsions. In adults, Epileptic fits are those
mostly met with, though apoplectic fits are not unknown. So
far as treatment is concerned, this differs with the kind of fit.
When puppies teething are the victims it is best to keep the
bowels acting freely ; while if the fits are due to worms the
eradication of these pests will of course be necessary.
Epileptic fits attack dogs very suddenly, and anyone
unacquainted with them might reasonably feel alarmed. A
dog when attacked falls over, struggling most violently, and
a frothy saliva comes from the mouth. Having removed
the animal to a quiet place and one of safety, it should be
allowed to remain until it recovers. This usually takes place
in a few minutes, the animal frequently appearing little the
worse for its experience. Violent exercise upon a heavy meal
may be productive of such a fit, or more frequently one of
an apoplectic character ; it may be due to worms, or to some
hereditary tendency, or it may be heralding an attack of
distemper. In the last case these fits are recurrent. Where
a dog remains unconscious more than a few minutes, if an
ordinary smelling-bottle can be procured and held to the
nostrils it will usually be of service. In adult dogs, when
the fits are persistent 5gr. to 20gr. of sodium bromide,
given in water, twice a day, will often check the fits or lessen
their frequency and severity.

Fleas.

Though perhaps not so objectionable as Lice these lively insects prevent the dog from taking that rest which is desirable; while, being also intermediaries of certain Tapeworms, they are very undesirable on that account. They are found on the dog as perfect insects only, the larval stage being passed in the dust, &c., that accumulates in kennels. A good bath in a solution of Izal will be found very beneficial. The strength for this is indicated by the makers. A spraying with spirits of camphor, followed by a combing over a vessel of water, will dislodge many of the pests in a half-stupefied condition, when they may be destroyed. Then, too, there are excellent shampoo washes sold by firms like Sherley and Bird and Storey, that are most useful in getting rid of these pests, while Garstin's Tonic Dog Soap is a first-class insecticide. All bedding and dust should be burnt, and the kennel or other sleeping-place treated to an insecticide. For kennels, Izal, Sanitas, or Jeyes' Fluid may be confidently recommended.

Indigestion.

A very common ailment among dogs is indigestion, which manifests itself in various ways—diarrhœa, constipation, foul breath, poor appetite, vomition of food, &c. Generally speaking, unsuitable foods and lack of proper exercise are responsible for the trouble. The remedy is fairly obvious. A couple of ordinary compound rhubarb pills will be found excellent in such cases. They may be given every other night for a week. Dogs suffering from indigestion will, moreover, develop a most unhealthy appetite, and devour all sorts of objectionable things, from cinders to human excreta. To allay the irritation of the stomach, after the cause has been removed, give 5gr. of subnitrate of bismuth, dry upon the tongue night and morning. If the breath is fœtid, give a pill night and morning composed of 1gr. to 3gr. of permanganate of potash.

Lice.

Though not perhaps so well-known as parasites of the dog as the humble flea, yet it is almost impossible for an owner to keep many dogs before he is acquainted with these parasites. Two widely different species of Lice affect the dog—the one a biting and the other a sucking insect. The former feeds chiefly on the skin excretions, and is not particularly harmful. The other is very objectionable, as it irritates and weakens its host very considerably. Moreover, it is an intermediary host of an undesirable Tapeworm. In dealing with these parasites, which are found alike upon adult dogs and puppies, not only has one to consider the Lice themselves, but the " nits " or egg-cases containing the unhatched generations. It is these that account for a dog, which a few days before appeared to be free, being teeming with Lice. The " nits " are affixed firmly to the hair-shafts, and are untouched by the remedies generally employed against the perfect insects. For these a little acetic acid carefully rubbed in will dissolve the egg. Heald, Spratt, Rackham, and Sherley all sell excellent preparations for combating these pests ; but they must be persistently employed. Where, however, a temporary or a home-made remedy is called for, olive-oil two parts and paraffin one part is as good as anything ; another is 1 in 50 of Jeyes' Fluid. Some people use the paraffin pure, but it is not advisable as a rule, though the skins of different dogs vary considerably as regards their sensitiveness. Ordinary dog soaps are useless against Lice. Not only, too, is it necessary to treat the dog, but its kennel should receive attention. All old bedding, combed-out hair, &c., should be burnt, and the kennel itself should be thoroughly cleansed with a first-class insecticide. Brushes and combs must also receive attention after each grooming, or reinfestation will speedily take place.

Mange.

Two forms of true mange are peculiar to the dog—Sarcoptic and Follicular. Both are due to the presence of minute parasites (not insects, as frequently stated) that invade the skin and cause much irritation. In the former the Mites burrow beneath the cuticle, and the latter beneath the hair follicles. Though Sarcoptic Mange is a difficult disease to combat, yet it is nothing like so difficult as the Black or Follicular variety, which must be left entirely to the skilled veterinary to treat. In the Sarcoptic form the parasites are found from head to tail. Though it is not easy without the aid of a glass to differentiate Sarcoptic Mange from certain forms of Eczema, yet an intelligent owner should be able to diagnose it. The disease is characterised by a falling out of the hair, by the presence of red pimples, and later by bladder-like pustules, in each of which there is a black speck. If neglected, these pustules burst, exuding a fluid, and completely rot the coat; they also coalesce, giving the dog a most unwholesome look. A dog suffering from Mange should be isolated from healthy occupants, and the kennel thoroughly disinfected. The dog may be treated with one of the many preparations upon the market—Rackham's, Spratt's, and Bird and Storey's being well known—or with olive oil 1 pint, oil of tar (oleum cadinum P.B.) 2oz., sulphur 3oz. He should be dressed all over twice a week for three weeks, then washed with Garstin's Tonic Dog Soap and hot water, and the dressing repeated if necessary. The less delay there is in its application, once the disease is diagnosed, the better, as it quickly spreads. If the disease is treated at once, an ointment composed of 1 part of ichthyol to 8 parts of vaseline is effective if used persistently and well rubbed in. Follicular Mange, like Sarcoptic, is characterised by great irritation and a shrinking of the skin. The disease is one that is not suitable for home treatment, as often many months of constant attention are necessary before a cure can be effected.

Red Mange.

A form of Eczema in which the skin, particularly that in the vicinity of the arms and thighs, takes on a red appearance, hence the popular name.

Rheumatism.

Sporting Terriers, and especially those which are called upon to work in the wet and damp for hours together, and

that probably receive scant treatment on their return to
kennels, are often afflicted with Rheumatism, more especially
that form known to the old kennel-men as Chest-Founder or
Kennel Lameness. Similarly, dogs that are kennelled on
damp ground are unusually prone to the disease. When
Kennel Lameness is the particular form of Rheumatism, it
will at once be noted that the parts in the vicinity of the
shoulder-blades are those affected. Another form of the
disease attacks the dog in the regions of the back. Usually
the first warning an owner gets that his dog is the subject of
Rheumatism is a crying-out given vent to when moving, or
when the parts affected are touched. This is perhaps accom-
panied by a local stiffness. Novices, however, are usually
puzzled at the way the disease seems to shift from one limb
to another. Accompanying the symptoms already referred to
are usually found a hot and dry nose, unpleasant breath, a
furred tongue, scanty and highly-coloured urine, and constipation. Having located the dog in a dry, airy kennel, and
moved the bowels freely by means of a couple of compound
rhubarb pills given every other night for a week, salicylate of
soda 10gr. given three times a day in an ounce of distilled
water should afford relief. When the soda fails to give
relief, give a pill, night and morning, containing 5gr. of
benzoic acid, in place of the soda. Hot baths also give
immediate relief very often. Keep the dog wrapped in
flannel afterwards, and indoors ; give a bath on alternate
days. A good embrocation, Sanitas for instance, may also
prove of benefit, though so painful sometimes is the affected
part that the rubbing thereof is a matter of difficulty. A light
dietary should be given, as naturally a dog so afflicted cannot
take exercise.

Rickets (Rachitis).

A very prevalent disease where puppies are reared under
improper conditions. Though chiefly an ailment of puppyhood, it is not absolutely so. The disease is due to a lack of
earthy matter in the bones, chiefly noticeable in the limbs (but

the spine and other osseous structures may be affected), which consequently bend under the weight, causing the joints to be misshapen and the legs bowed. Puppies that are much inbred, reared in stuffy kennels, and fed upon an unsuitable dietary are oftenest the victims. Cows' milk, which is usually given, is a very poor substitute for the milk of the dam, and puppies reared thereon suffer accordingly. Lactol and Malt Milk Food are preparations that should be employed in the rearing of puppies directly they are fit to leave the dam. Where puppies are "walked" in pairs, Rickets less often makes its appearance. Once the legs have become bowed there is no cure, and necessarily such animals, which are also usually more or less of wastrels, are not worth the trouble of rearing. Phosphate of calcium in 10gr. doses, given in the food twice a day for a few weeks, should prove beneficial. On no account should rickety parents be bred from.

Ringworm.

A disease due to a specific fungus, and one that may be readily transmitted from cattle to dogs and even to man. There are two varieties, characterised by the manner in which the surface skin is affected—honeycomb or circular. The disease is one that requires alike prompt and careful treatment. One of the best preparations is oleate of copper (or yellow mercuric oxide) ointment, first washing the affected part with soap and water. A dog suffering from Ringworm should be at once isolated from its kennel companions, the bedding burnt, and the kennel thoroughly disinfected with Izal, Sanitas, or Jeyes' Fluid.

Sore Feet.

In the preparation that Terriers required for show have to undergo—namely, plenty of road exercise—the pads of the feet are very liable to suffer. When this is the case the dog should cease to be so exercised, and the feet bathed in a wine-red solution of Condy's Fluid; or allowed to stand in a saturated solution of alum, or in 1 in 60 of warm Jeyes', afterwards well dried and anointed with pitch ointment. Foreign substances are also readily picked up, and the feet must therefore be periodically examined, and thorns, pieces of flint, &c., removed with a pair of tweezers. Again, it is not at all uncommon for an eczematous condition to be responsible for soreness between the toes (referred to under Eczema). In this case, when the cause is removed the effect will cease.

Ticks.

Terriers that are used for working amidst herbage and vegetation generally are very liable to be infested with Ticks, which attach themselves to their hosts and gorge themselves on their blood. Naturally, they induce considerable irritation and not a little weakness. Ordinary insecticides are not of any use against these Spider-like animals (they are not insects), and recourse must therefore be had to other measures to get rid of the pests. If but a few exist they may be lightly touched with a camel-hair brush dipped in methylated spirit or in turps; the creatures will then relax their hold and fall to the ground, when they may be crushed. Where, however, the dogs are badly infested, paraffin and olive-oil, as advised for Lice, will be found efficacious, as will Heald's Tick Lotion or the preparation sold by Rackham or Spratt's Patent. It is inadvisable to attempt to pull out the Ticks, as, the mouth-parts being firmly embedded, they are very liable to be left in the dog, causing a nasty sore.

Worms.

So numerous are these internal parasites of the dog that to deal at all exhaustively with them would entail considerable space. All that can be said is that all are very undesirable, and many are extremely harmful to their hosts. Roundworms, Tapeworms, and Threadworms are all found in the dog, Tapeworms being the most numerous as to species, as they are the most objectionable; while some are not only undesirable because of their associations with the dog, but by reason of the fact that one stage of their life-history is passed in some other domestic or other animal used for food. Take the commonest of all the Tapeworms infesting the dog, *Tænia cænurus.* This in the cyst stage is found in the brain of the sheep, and is responsible for the disease known as " Gid," or " Turnside." From this it will at once be obvious that it is to the interest of the farmer and the stock-owner to see that all dogs kept on their establishments are free from this Tapeworm, otherwise they will be scattering the ova of such pests over pastures on which sheep are browsing, to their certain detriment.

Little by way of description is needed to differentiate the different sections of worms that infest the dog, the very names—Round, Tape, and Thread—being sufficiently suggestive. The first are frequently harboured by puppies, and may vary in length from less than an inch to six inches and more. It is necessary to know which kind of worm is being harboured, in order that the correct vermifuge may be employed. For instance, while areca-nut constitutes an excellent vermifuge in the case of Round-Worms, it is by itself not of much avail in the case of Tapeworms. An owner, however, having satisfied himself as to the existence of the one or the other, is in the best of positions for dealing with the parasites. The number of firms making vermifuges a speciality is very great. Well-tried remedies, however, are those put up by Heald, Naldire, Spratt's Patent, Bird and Storey, and Rackham. So far as Tapeworms are concerned, we have found oil of male fern most efficacious when given on a fasting stomach; but, being so nauseous, it is best administered in capsule form. These capsules are obtainable with doses suited to every class of dog. For Round or Thread Worms 2gr. of santonin every other day for three days should prove effective. It should be given fasting and followed in twelve hours with a dessert-spoonful of castor oil.

Dogs that are infested with worms have a generally unthrifty appearance—thin, with a staring coat—a capricious or, it may be, an inordinate appetite, may have fits, an irritable skin, indigestion, &c. Periodically we think it is advisable to give a vermifuge, even if there be no decided evidences of worms, as the drugs employed, if administered with care, cannot do any harm, and they may be productive of a vast amount of good.   For puppies, say six months old, Sherley's Worm Capsules are excellent in every way.

INDEX.

k

L. UPCOTT GILL, LONDON & COUNTY PRINTING WORKS, LONDON, W.C.

Lightning Source UK Ltd.
Milton Keynes UK
02 January 2009

148106UK00001B/23/A